# The Evolution and Determinants of Wealth Inequality in the North Atlantic Anglo-Sphere, 1668–2013

Livio Di Matteo

# The Evolution and Determinants of Wealth Inequality in the North Atlantic Anglo-Sphere, 1668–2013

Push and Pull

palgrave
macmillan

Livio Di Matteo
Department of Economics
Lakehead University
Thunder Bay, ON, Canada

ISBN 978-3-319-89772-1 ISBN 978-3-319-89773-8 (eBook)
https://doi.org/10.1007/978-3-319-89773-8

Library of Congress Control Number: 2018938196



Printed on acid-free paper

This Palgrave Pivot imprint is published by the registered company Springer International Publishing AG part of Springer Nature.
The registered company address is: Gewerbestrasse 11, 6330 Cham, Switzerland

*To Olivia and Nicholas*
*The twenty-first century belongs to them.*

# Contents

# List of Figures

# List of Tables

CHAPTER 1

# An Unequal World: Introduction to Wealth Inequality in the North Atlantic Anglosphere

**Abstract** Economic inequality is a key research area, and the direction of the relationship between industrialization, economic growth, and economic inequality over time is a key question. An examination of wealth inequality in the north Atlantic Anglosphere countries of Canada, the United Kingdom, and the United States from 1668 to 2013 finds that the process of economic growth and industrialization has pushed wealth inequality upwards while other economic factors have either reinforced inequality or pulled it down. While wealth inequality is generally high, it declined over the long term and, unlike income inequality, has not experienced as pronounced a rebound in these or other developed countries since the mid-twentieth century—with the notable exception of the United States.

**Keywords** Wealth • Inequality • Industrialization • Push • Pull

*Acknowledgements*: The author wishes to thank Daniel Waldenström and Jeffrey Williamson for their comments on earlier versions of this project. As well, portions of this project were delivered at conferences and seminars and received helpful comments. These venues included the Social Sciences History Meetings, Chicago, November 17–20, 2016, the Seminar Series, University of Economics (VSE), Prague, October 12, 2016 and the Meetings of the Canadian Economic Association, Ottawa, June 2–5, 2016.



L. Di Matteo, *The Evolution and Determinants of Wealth Inequality in the North Atlantic Anglo-Sphere, 1668–2013*,
https://doi.org/10.1007/978-3-319-89773-8_1

Economic inequality, with its effects and policy implications, is now a leading topic of scrutiny in social science research as well as media attention. One only needs to witness the widespread media coverage that accompanies the release of international asset distribution data such as the global wealth reports done by Credit Suisse.[1] It is an issue that increasingly dominates economic history and current policy as evidenced by the work of scholars like Thomas Piketty (2014)[2] and the incessant global preoccupation with the wealth and income shares of the top 1 percent of distributions.[3] Indeed, the concern with inequality receives further impetus as additional research also generates empirical links between economic inequality and social outcomes such as homicide rates and health status.[4]

Piketty's provocative thesis that lower economic growth rates combined with a rate of return to capital and assets greater than the rate of economic growth generate growing inequality is pessimistic. It is certainly a more ominous result for long-term human economic welfare when compared to the sunnier Kuznets curve hypothesis of slowing post-industrialization growth and greater economic equality. On the other hand, other research suggests that the dispersion and mean of inequality across countries, at pre-industrial times and today, are actually similar, suggesting there actually has been little long-term change when it comes to inequality.[5]

Indeed, it would seem the direction of the relationship between industrialization, economic growth, and economic inequality over time is a key question. Moreover, all of this work also suggests that the initial conditions and economic and political institutions of a society matter for the long-term structure and evolution of its national wealth holding as well as the impact of explicit government policies in affecting these distributions.[6] Yet, ultimately, any significant understanding of the long-term structure and evolution of inequality requires the methodical and consistent compilation of reliable long-term data.

This empirical contribution focuses on wealth inequality trends in the North Atlantic Anglosphere[7] countries of Canada, the United Kingdom, and the United States over the period from 1668 to 2013—a longer-term perspective than generally used when wealth inequality is discussed. It is important to put current dimensions of wealth inequality into historical context by looking at performance over the long run that involves centuries rather than simply a few decades. More importantly, this contribution compiles a substantial amount of data on estimates of wealth inequality.

Over the course of nearly four centuries, the process of economic change, growth, and industrialization has generally served to push wealth inequality upward, while an assortment of other economic factors, shocks, and policy responses have either worked to reinforce the upward trend or served to mitigate inequality by pulling it back down. While wealth inequality is generally high, it has declined over the long term and, unlike income inequality, has not been experiencing as pronounced of an international rebound in the developed countries since the mid-twentieth century—with the notable exception of the United States. Indeed, the American experience with respect to rising wealth inequality is different not only from European countries but also with respect to its Atlantic Anglosphere compatriots of Canada and the United Kingdom.

An advantage of using these North Atlantic Anglosphere countries is that they share commonalities across history, political structure, language, institutions, and economic as well as cultural features, given the original colonial relationships shared by both Canada and the United States with respect to Great Britain. All three of these countries have been at the forefront of economic development with high levels of real per capita GDP as well as high rates of economic growth.[8] This allows for a comparison of trends, with more focus on long-term policy, with political and societal choices as additional factors determining differences in the evolution of wealth inequality—in a sense, a more controlled historical experiment.

There are also important economic links between these countries, especially with respect to Canada and both the United States and the United Kingdom. Prior to the Great Depression, Canada's most important trade partner was the United Kingdom, whereas by the end of the twentieth century, it was the United States. In 1900, 54 percent of total Canadian exports were to the United Kingdom while 36 percent were to the United States.[9] By the early twenty-first century, Canada's exports to the United States had grown to account for nearly 80 percent of its exports, whereas those to the United Kingdom had declined to about 3 percent.[10]

Canadian trade with the United States grew during the course of the twentieth century to account for two-thirds of its exports by 1970, but then accelerated with the onset of free trade during the 1980s. Despite increasing economic integration with the United States via Canada-US Free Trade in 1988 and the North American Free Trade Agreement (NAFTA) that started in 1994, which many felt might lead to harmonization of social policies, Canada has been able to chart a separate path on social and redistributive policy, which may be a factor in explaining its wealth inequality experience.

There are of course also some notable economic and political differences. For example, both Canada and the United States are characterized as federations with a substantial degree of economic and political power decentralized away from the federal governments, while the United Kingdom until the mid-twentieth century has been more of a unitary state. As well, both Canada and the United States began their development as more resource-intensive export economies prior to developing their manufacturing sectors, whereas the United Kingdom moved from an agricultural-commercial economy to industrialization and global empire.[11] Indeed, as the first industrial nation, the United Kingdom was unique in its experience of industrialization as it became the world's preeminent exporter of manufactured goods and then a source of international capital in the nineteenth century.[12]

The development of the American economy began with natural resource exports that included tobacco, rice, cotton, corn, wheat, and indigo. Later on, this was accompanied by a process of Western frontier expansion and agricultural settlement as well as manufacturing development and urbanization, especially in the Northeast. Moreover, the share of US exports accounted for by natural resources remained high in the nineteenth century and, indeed, well into the early twentieth century, while natural resources in general continued as important inputs into its manufacturing development.[13]

Canada's economic development started with exports of fish, fur, and lumber, as well as agricultural settlement culminating with prairie settlement and the wheat export boom, urbanization, and manufacturing development. However, natural resources have continued as an important contributor to the Canadian economy—even more so than the United States—with estimates suggesting that as much as one-fifth of the Canadian economy relies on natural resources either directly or indirectly.[14] Moreover, a key distinction with respect to Canadian natural resources relative to the United States is the long tradition of greater public ownership of natural resources as well as the historically high rate of foreign ownership.[15]

The questions to be examined in this study are as follows. First, given the available evidence, what are the long-term trends in wealth inequality in Canada, the United States, and the United Kingdom, and how do these three countries differ in terms of both the level of and trends in wealth inequality. This evidence is collected largely from historical micro-data studies that have been done for all three countries over time and on its own represents an important inventory of inequality data and results.

Second, was inequality correlated with industrialization in these three countries, and why did lower inequality often characterize the more agriculturally intensive phases of their economies? Third, was inequality in the twentieth century mitigated by government policy responses? Fourth, given the historical, institutional, cultural, and language similarities between Canada, the United States, and the United Kingdom, what explains the differences in wealth inequality over time?

A combination of basic inequality measures, raw data sources, and published wealth inequality estimates is used, including own estimates from original micro-data. The results show high and rising wealth inequality in all three countries during industrialization in the nineteenth century, with a decline during the twentieth century. Evidence for Canada and the United States shows rising wealth inequality beginning after the 1970s especially for the United States and an arrest in the decline in Canadian inequality.

The level of Canadian wealth inequality in general has been more muted relative to either the United States or the United Kingdom. Indeed, Canada appears to be somewhat of an outlier in terms of the level of inequality, changes in inequality, as well as its volatility over time. Is this a result of natural resource intensity, the effects of technology and domestic saving, or a social contract of sorts? Some evidence suggests that differences in rates of home ownership as well as trade unionization may be factors here.

The rise in wealth inequality also coincides with changes in estate and death tax regimes in these countries that reduced their impact, suggesting that these taxes may have indeed played some role in affecting the distribution of wealth, but the evidence is mixed. At the same time, despite parallel changes to the system of estate taxation in the United Kingdom during this time, there is not as pronounced an upsurge in wealth inequality. Here, a significant factor appears to be the mitigating effect of 'Right to Buy' policies as a result of the passing of the Housing Act of 1980, which led to an increase in home ownership.

## Notes

1. The *Global Wealth Report 2017* done by Credit Suisse analyzed the wealth held by 4.8 billion adults around the world. See: https://www.credit-suisse.com/corporate/en/research/research-institute/global-wealth-report.html
2. See Piketty (1992, 2000, 2014), and Piketty et al. (2006). See also Roine and Waldenström (2015), Piketty and Saez (2003), Saez and Veall (2005).

3. See, for example, Yalnizyan (2010), Wolff (2010), Oxfam (2015), Macdonald (2014), Jackson (2015), Freund and Oliver (2016), and Waldenström (2017). For a recent historical paper, see Bengtsson et al. (2016).
4. Daly (2016) presents a link between inequality and homicides by arguing that economic inequality is the cause of social problems that elicit greater violence, particularly among males. Subramanian and Kawachi (2004) and Lynch et al. (2001) draw the link between income inequality and higher mortality rates.
5. See Milanovic et al. (2010).
6. See Waldenström (2017).
7. The Anglosphere is rooted in the British Empire and generally refers to the network and close association of English-speaking common-law-based countries. It can be defined as narrowly as the United States, the United Kingdom, Canada, Australia, and New Zealand but more broadly can also include many current and former members of the British Empire and Commonwealth. For a discussion, see Bennett (2007), Willetts (2007), and Kenny and Pearce (2015).
8. For some overviews of historical economic growth and development in these countries, see Urquhart (1993), Gordon (2016), and Broadberry (2015).
9. Firestone (1960; Table 3).
10. Data source: Statistics Canada, Table 2280001, Series v191490, v191559 and v191560.
11. Models of export-led development rooted in resource extraction are referred to as Staples models. For accounts of Canadian and US economic history in the Staples tradition, see Watkins (1963), Innis (1930), McCusker and Menard (1985), and North (1961).
12. For a classic account, see Ashton (Ashton 1961). See also Broadberry (2015) and Floud and Johnson (2004, 2008).
13. See Vanek (1963), who notes that raw materials and crude foods still accounted for 25 percent of US exports in 1945. Moreover, Gavin Wright (1990) argues that the resource intensity of American manufacturing exports was increasing between 1880 and 1920. For overviews of American economic development, see Atack and Passell (1994) and Engerman and Gallman (1996, 2000a, b).
14. Natural resources have been an important driver of general Canadian economic prosperity. For a classic account, see Innis (1930). For Canada, Keay (2007) finds that the exploitation of Canada's natural resources during the twentieth century made direct and indirect contributions to the size and efficiency of the Canadian economy and had a substantial positive impact on the level of real per capita GDP, contributing about 20 percent. Another comprehensive study by Baldwin and MacDonald (2012) also finds natural resources and trade to be important contributors to Canadian real gross national income between 1870 and 2010.
15. Piketty (2014: 158).

## References

Ashton, T. S. (1961/1948). *The Industrial Revolution*. London: Oxford University Press.

Atack, J., & Passell, P. (1994). *A New Economic View of American History: From Colonial Times to 1940* (2nd ed.). New York: Norton.

Baldwin, J. R., & MacDonald, R. (2012). *Natural Resources, the Terms of Trade, and Real Income Growth in Canada: 1870 to 2010*. Statistics Canada, Economic Analysis (EA) Research Paper Series, No. 11F0027M—No. 7.

Bengtsson, E., Missiaia, A., Olsson, M., & Svenson, P. (2016, November). *The Wealth of the Richest: Inequality and the Nobility in Sweden, 1750–1900*. Paper Presented at the Social Science History Meetings, Chicago.

Bennett, J. C. (2007). *The Anglosphere Challenge. Why English-Speaking Nations Will Lead the Way in the Twenty-First Century*. New York: Rowman and Littlefield.

Broadberry, S. (2015). *British Economic Growth, 1270–1870*. Cambridge: Cambridge University Press.

Daly, M. (2016). *Killing the Competition: Economic Inequality and Homicide*. New York: Routledge.

Engerman, S. L., & Gallman, R. E. (1996). *The Cambridge Economic History of the United States. Volume I. The Colonial Era*. Cambridge: Cambridge University Press.

Engerman, S. L., & Gallman, R. E. (2000a). *The Cambridge Economic History of the United StatesVolume II. The Long Nineteenth Century*. Cambridge: Cambridge University Press.

Engerman, S. L., & Gallman, R. E. (2000b). *The Cambridge Economic History of the United States. Volume III. The Twentieth Century*. Cambridge: Cambridge University Press.

Firestone, O. J. (1960). *Canada's External Trade and Net Foreign Balance, 1851–1900*. Trends in the American Economy in the Nineteenth Century, The Conference on Research in Income and Wealth, Princeton University Press, pp. 757–771. http://www.nber.org/chapters/c11719

Floud, R., & Johnson, P. (Eds.). (2004). *The Cambridge Economic History of Modern Britain. Volume 1. Industrialization, 1700–1860*. Cambridge: Cambridge University Press.

Floud, R., & Johnson, P. (Eds.). (2008). *The Cambridge Economic History of Modern Britain. Volume 2. Economic Maturity, 1860 to 1939*. Cambridge: Cambridge University Press.

Freund, C., & Oliver, S. (2016). *The Origins of the Superrich: The Billionaire Characteristics Database, Working Paper Series* (Vol. 16-1). Washington, DC: Peterson Institute for International Economics.

Gordon, R. J. (2016). *The Rise and Fall of American Growth*. Princeton: Princeton University Press.

Innis, H. A. (1930). The Importance of Staple Products. In W. T. Easterbrook & M. H. Watkins (Eds.), *Approaches to Canadian Economic History*. Toronto: McClelland and Stewart, 1967.

Jackson, A. (2015, April 8). *The Return of the Gilded Age: Consequences, Causes and Solutions*. Broadbent Institute, The Harry Kitchen Lecture in Public Policy.

Keay, I. (2007). The Engine or the Caboose? Resource Industries and Twentieth-Century Canadian Economic Performance. *The Journal of Economic History, 67*(1), 1–32.

Kenny, M., & Pearce, N. (2015, February 10). *The Rise of the Anglosphere: How the Right Dreamed Up a New World Order*. New Statesman. http://www.newstatesman.com/politics/2015/02/rise-anglosphere-how-right-dreamed-new-conservative-world-order

Lynch, J., Smith, G. D., Hillemeier, M., Shaw, M., Raghunathan, T., & Kaplan, G. (2001). Income Inequality, the Psychosocial Environment, and Health: Comparisons of Wealthy Nations. *The Lancet, 358*(9277), 194–200.

Macdonald, D. (2014, April). *Outrageous Fortune: Documenting Canada's Wealth Gap*. Canadian Centre for Policy Alternatives.

McCusker, J. J., & Menard, R. R. (1985). *The Economy of British North America*. Chapel Hill: University of North Carolina Press.

Milanovic, B., Lindert, P. H., & Williamson, J. G. (2010). Pre-Industrial Inequality. *The Economic Journal, 121*(March), 255–272.

North, D. C. (1961). *The Economic Growth of the United States, 1790–1860*. Englewood Cliffs: Prentice-Hall.

Oxfam. (2015, January). *Wealth: Having It All and Wanting More*. Oxfam Issue Briefing.

Piketty, T. (1992). *Imperfect Capital Markets and Persistence of Initial Wealth Inequalities*. Discussion Paper No. TE/92/255, Suntory Centre, London School of Economics and Political Science.

Piketty, T. (2000). Theories of Persistent Inequality and Intergenerational Mobility. In A. B. Atkinson & F. Bourguignon (Eds.), *Handbook of Income Distribution* (Vol. I, pp. 429–476). Amsterdam: Elsevier Science.

Piketty, T. (2014). *Capital in the 21st Century*. Cambridge, MA: Harvard University Press.

Piketty, T., & Saez, E. (2003). Income Inequality in the United States, 1913–1998. *The Quarterly Journal of Economics, CXVIII*(1), 1–39.

Piketty, T., Postel-Vinay, G., & Rosenthal, J.-L. (2006). Wealth Concentration in a Developing Economy: Paris and France, 1807–1994. *American Economic Review, 96*(1), 236–256.

Roine, J., & Waldenström, D. (2015). Long-Run Trends in the Distribution of Income and Wealth. In A. B. Atkinson & F. Bourguignon (Eds.), *Handbook of Income Distribution* (Vol. 2A, pp. 469–592). Amsterdam: Elsevier.

Saez, E., & Veall, M. (2005). The Evolution of High Incomes in Northern America: Lessons from Canadian Evidence. *American Economic Review, 95*, 831–849.

Subramanian, S. V., & Kawachi, I. (2004). Income Inequality and Health: What We Have Learned So Far. *Epidemiologic Reviews, 26*(1), 78–91.

Urquhart, M. C. (1993). *Gross National Product, Canada 1870 to 1926*. Montreal: McGill-Queen's University Press.

Vanek, J. (1963). *The Natural Resource Content of United States Foreign Trade, 1870–1955*. Cambridge, MA: MIT Press.

Waldenström, D. (2017). Wealth-Income Ratios in a Small, Developing Economy: Sweden, 1810–2014. *Journal of Economic History, 77*(1), 285–313.

Watkins, M. H. (1963). A Staple Theory of Economic Growth. *The Canadian Journal of Economics and Political Science, 24*, 141–158.

Willetts, D. (2007). England and Britain, Europe and the Anglosphere. *The Political Quarterly, 78*(1), 54–61.

Wolff, E. N. (2010, March). *Recent Trends in household Wealth in the United States: Rising Debt and the Middle Class Squeeze-an Update to 2007*. Levy Economics Institute. Working Paper No. 589.

Wright, G. (1990). The Origins of American Industrial Success, 1879–1940. *American Economic Review, 80*, 651–668.

Yalnizyan, A. (2010, December). *The Rise of Canada's Richest 1%*. Canadian Center for Policy Alternatives.

CHAPTER 2

# Wealth Inequality and Its Historical Context

**Abstract** Wealth inequality is the disparity in asset ownership. Wealth provides more economic security than income and is a better indicator of economic and political power. The long-term impact of industrialization and growth in the Kuznets Curve Hypothesis postulates an optimistic inverted u-shaped inequality-growth relationship, as opposed to Piketty's pessimism. Evidence supports and contradicts the Kuznets curve and finds additional economic, technological, demographic, social, and institutional factors affecting the long-term distribution of both wealth and income. On balance, the studies conducted suggest that economic inequality was relatively lower in pre-industrial periods, grew during industrialization, and then appears to have been mitigated in the wake of industrialization with the advent of social security, public policy, and social investments that may have broadened wealth accumulation opportunities.

**Keywords** Kuznets • Technology • Piketty • Wealth shares

Wealth inequality can be simply defined as the disparity in the ownership of assets, and it differs from disparities in the earning of income. Much of the work on economic inequality has focused on income, but it has been argued that economic inequality is indeed multi-dimensional, with income,



L. Di Matteo, *The Evolution and Determinants of Wealth Inequality in the North Atlantic Anglo-Sphere, 1668–2013*,
https://doi.org/10.1007/978-3-319-89773-8_2

consumption and wealth both independently and jointly determining inequality.[1] While much current research focuses on income, some economists also prefer consumption as an estimate of permanent income, while Fisher et al. (2016b) argue that wealth in many respects is an excellent measure of economic welfare because it allows for the ability to affect both income and consumption quite directly.

Indeed, as noted by Fisher et al. (2016a: 22), 'wealth is a stock that can be used to stabilize consumption in times of misfortune, or to increase realized income flows' and in the long term can even provide a dynastic advantage to maintaining economic and social position. Indeed, this makes a case for a heavier weighting on wealth rather than income when it comes to understanding the long-term evolution of economic inequality. As well, Meyer and Sullivan (2017) note that income inequality statistics may not accurately reflect total economic inequality because income is often poorly measured in the tails of the income distribution and may not capture consumption paid for via borrowing, such as that for consumer durables.

In terms of historical work, studies have focused on both wealth and income over time, and since wealth and income are correlated, they are indeed often used interchangeably in discussions of historical inequality. They are however quite different, given that wealth is a stock at a point in time whereas income is a flow over a period of time. Unlike wealth, income can often reflect a direct and more immediate return to human capital. Moreover, the return to wealth can be a source of income independent of wage earnings, which is a return to human capital. However, as already noted, large stocks of wealth may provide more economic security than income, which is more dependent on wage income and can be affected by employment loss. They also differ in that wealth is sometimes considered a better measure of economic and ultimately political power in a society, while income better reflects current standards of living.[2]

Whether long-term economic development and industrialization reduced or increased income and wealth inequality is still debated with the seminal work being that of Simon Kuznets. The invariably optimistic Kuznets curve hypothesis maintains that inequality grew during the rapid economic growth of industrialization and then declined once industrialization spread and the economic growth rate slowed, generating an inverted u-shaped curve between inequality and growth.[3] However, recent literature questions the optimism of this view with respect to both income and wealth inequality along with the timing of growth and industrialization, especially given studies from new regions and time periods.[4] Moreover, there are concerns that the Kuznets curve relationship needs to take other confounding factors into account.[5]

While there are abundant regional and national studies of economic inequality at points in time, integrative long-term views of wealth inequality across countries have been less frequent, though recent years have seen a move toward the compilation of new data on long-term trends. As Davies and Shorrocks (2000) note, it is well known that wealth is generally more unequally distributed than income[6] and that there has been some reduction in wealth inequality since the end of the nineteenth century.

Piketty (2014) in particular mobilizes an impressive quantity of data for trends in the inequality of capital and income—over the course of several hundred years—for developed countries such as France, the United States, Canada, Britain, Australia, Sweden, Japan, Italy, Spain, and Denmark, as well as a number of emerging countries.[7] Piketty finds a decline in inequality moving into the twentieth century and then a reversal after the middle of the century. Arrondel and Grange (2003, 2006, 2014) have done substantial work on long-term wealth and inequality trends in France focusing on wealth transmission, and results show that the generational immobility of wealth in the nineteenth and early twentieth centuries was significant.

Milanovic (2016) argues that economic inequality moves in broad cycles as a result of long-term Kuznets waves, with the current rise in inequality being driven by a new Kuznets wave of innovation in both technology and trade that is generating economic growth and change. Industrialization was also tandem with a Kuznets wave of technological advance and globalization that then generated countervailing forces such as increased educational attainment and political upheaval that served to reduce inequality to the lows achieved by the 1970s.

Williamson and Lindert[8] maintain that industrialization in the United States increased inequality. Lindert and Williamson (2012, 2016) show rising income inequality in the United States in particular moved in two waves—from 1774 to 1860 coinciding with early industrialization and then again from the 1970s to the present. On the other hand, Soltow[9] was inclined to believe that the industrial revolution reduced inequality because the factory revolution fostered economic diversification and offered greater employment opportunities than had previously existed. Yet, even Soltow himself noted that eighteenth-century America exhibited significant wealth inequality that was nevertheless tolerated because of wider rates of property holding relative to Europe.[10]

Indeed, high rates of growth in property holding were a feature particularly of European settler economies despite the high inequality. North American studies of wealth during the nineteenth and early twentieth centuries find robust annual rates of asset accumulation as well as high degrees of wealth inequality, even in frontier areas of recent settlement.[11] Similarly, Australia and New Zealand as regions of recent European settler migration also demonstrated high levels of wealth inequality in the nineteenth century and early part of the twentieth century.[12] European studies also find quite high wealth inequality in the eighteenth and nineteenth centuries with some reduction over the course of the twentieth century.[13]

While some of these studies have examined change over time with an effort to seeing the effects of economic growth on inequality, the emphasis of many of these wealth micro-data studies is on measuring inequality at specific points in time or change over time in a specific region. Indeed, recent regional wealth inequality studies by Alfani and Ryckbosch (2016) and Alfani and Ammannati (2017) have found that medieval and early modern economic inequality even grew in the centuries prior to industrialization and cannot solely be explained by economic growth. The suggestion is that presence of representative political institutions, and relatively progressive fiscal systems with higher social spending, might also account for some of the regional variations in inequality.

Some long-term examinations of wealth inequality are of particular interest given the comparisons being pursued in this study. Wolff and Marley (1989) using individual based estate data estimate a decline in wealth concentration in the United States from the late 1920s to the late 1940s, a slight increase in the 1960s, a sharp drop in the 1970s, and then a minor increase to 1981. They also find that including social security wealth in the household portfolio increases the decline in inequality over the period 1939–1981, while changing the unit of observation in the estate data, from individual to household, reduces the decline in wealth concentration over the period 1922–1953, but not in the 1970s.

Shammas (1993: 428) argues that some of the additional factors affecting wealth inequality involve changes in property laws, including the legal emancipation of women along with the advent of liberal government programs in the wake of the Depression and World War II. Looking at select measures of wealth inequality using probate, census, and survey records, for the years 1774, 1860, 1870, and 1962, Shammas (1993) finds that the evolution of inequality measures for the United States also can vary depending on whether one measures inequality based on the adult population or households.

In addition, Shammas notes the wealth share of the top 1 percent appears to be subject to short-term fluctuations rather than a steady decline.[14] Indeed, the wealth share claimed by the top 1 and 5 percent of households appears higher in the late twentieth century than in 1774. What is perhaps the most remarkable according to Shammas is indeed 'how little wealth in any period has been owned by the majority of households, those in the bottom three quintiles'.[15] Moreover, what wealth has trickled down has generally come not from the top 1 percent but rather those placed lower in the top quintile. These results suggest that inequality has been especially ingrained in terms of the persistent lower wealth shares of the bottom half of the distribution.

Roine and Waldenström (2015) review long-run developments in the distribution of wealth and income starting from circa 1750—the time of the start of the British industrial take-off—for about ten developed countries[16] and find that wealth inequality was high and fairly constant in the nineteenth century. However, wealth inequality decreased during the first 80 years of the twentieth century almost everywhere, with the subsequent years marked by divergent trends across countries.

Roine and Waldenstrom find that the estimated top wealth shares at the beginning of the twentieth century are clearly higher in the United Kingdom relative to the United States, but starting around World War I, the wealth shares of top percentile groups decrease substantially. This decline continues until approximately 1980 when they generally stop falling for most countries. Wealth concentration generally declines in many of the other countries they examine after 1900 including the United Kingdom, but the United States is also an exception here given that the decline is not as steep.

Roine and Waldenstrom also find using a set of 26 developed countries[17] that income inequality as measured by the top 1 percent share of incomes fell from approximately World War I until the late 1970s and then grew. However, much of the increase in income inequality is driven by the Anglo-Saxon countries (including Canada, the United Kingdom, and the United States) and, to a lesser extent, the Asian (except Japan, which is flat) and the Nordic countries, as the Continental European countries do not demonstrate this trend.

For the United Kingdom, estimates going back for the period prior to 1800 done by Lindert (1986, 2000) and Soltow (1981) using probate and tax assessment records find high and increasing wealth inequality in the second half of the eighteenth century, with the nineteenth century also seeing increasing concentration at the top of the distribution. After World War I, work using estate tax data by Atkinson and Harrison (1978) and Atkinson et al. (1989) finds a steep drop in wealth inequality until the 1980s and then the start of an increase. Atkinson (2013) finds that inherited wealth as a share of national income fell from World War I until the 1970s but has since grown.

Studies documenting the long-term evolution of wealth in Canada are both less numerous and more compressed in their time-span. Hamilton et al. (2017: 1649) note that a remarkably detailed historical picture of wealth and inequality in Canada from the latter half of the nineteenth century and early part of the twentieth century has been constructed by Di Matteo. For 1892–1902, Di Matteo (2016) finds the wealth of the top 10 percent ranges from 72.6 to 80.9 percent, while that of the middle 40 percent ranges from 19.1 to 20.5 percent and the bottom 50 percent from 0 to 7 percent.

By 1984, the wealth (net worth) of the top 10 percent is down to 51.9 percent, that of the middle 40 percent rises to 42.2 percent, but the share of the bottom 50 percent is only 6 percent. By 2005, the share of the top 10 percent rebounds to 60.1 percent, while that of the middle 40 percent falls to 35.5 percent and that of the bottom 50 percent declines to 4.4 percent. Additional studies using Statistics Canada Survey of Consumer Finance and Survey of Financial Security Data find an increase in Canadian wealth inequality since the early 1980s[18] after a period of decline that marked the late 1960s and early 1970s.[19]

In summary, the balance of the numerous studies conducted suggests economic inequality was relatively lower in pre-industrial periods, grew during industrialization, and then appears to have been mitigated in the wake of industrialization. Wealth concentration diminished during the twentieth century, with the advent of social security and increased public sector spending and social investment as factors that appear to have increased opportunities for wealth accumulation for a broader range of population. Other factors that appear correlated with changes in wealth distribution were demographic and technological change, tax policy, labor supply, globalization and trade, and capital accumulation over time along with the impact of world war and Great Depression era.[20] However, there has been a resurgence of wealth and income inequality particularly in the United States during the latter part of the twentieth century.[21]

## Notes

1. See Fisher et al. (2016a, b). They note that inequality has increased since 1989 in all three of these dimensions. At the same time, research has also found that the increase in consumption inequality has not been as dramatic as income inequality. Krueger and Perri (2006) find that the recent increase in US income inequality has not been accompanied by a corresponding rise in consumption inequality.
2. Shammas (1993: 415). Indeed, Shammas (1993: 427) argues that the tenacious hold of the top 1 percent on a quarter to one third of total American wealth has been a force in political continuity. Reeves (2017) would broaden the tenacious political class to the top 20 percent in terms of income distribution—the so-called upper middle class.
3. Kuznets (1955, 1966).
4. Lindert and Williamson (2016). See also Abad and Junquera (2017), Alfani and Ryckbosch (2016), Reis (2016), and Malinowski and van Zanden (2016).
5. See Higgins and Williamson (2002) for a discussion.
6. Davies and Shorrocks (1999: 3). Evidence for the late twentieth century suggests Gini coefficients for income in developed countries range from 0.3 to 0.4, while for wealth the range is 0.5–0.9. See also Davies et al. (2011: 224) who 'find that intra-country inequality is so much larger in the case of wealth that it accounts for a larger share of global inequality than it does for income, according to the Gini coefficient. Thus it appears that a principal reason for the high global inequality of wealth may be the long-recognized high inequality of wealth within countries.'
7. For example, India, Indonesia, China, South Africa, and Columbia.
8. See Lindert (1991), Lindert and Williamson (1985), and Williamson and Lindert (1980).
9. Soltow (1989: 5).
10. The case that wealth inequality increases during industrialization is not supported unambiguously is also noted by Ohlsson et al. (2008), who find that wealth inequality in Denmark, Sweden, and Norway did not rise during their early industrialization.
11. For Canada: Siddiq, 'Size Distribution' (1988), Osberg/Siddiq, 'Inequality' (1993), Osberg/Siddiq, 'Wealth' (1993), Darroch, 'Industrialization' (1983), Siddiq/Gwyn, 'Importance' (1991), Di Matteo/George, 'Canadian Wealth' (1992), Di Matteo/George, 'Patterns' (1998), Gwyn/Siddiq, 'Wealth Distribution' (1992), Darroch/Soltow, *Property* (1994), Bouchard, 'Economic Inequalities' (1998), Baskerville, 'Women' (1999), For the United States: Gallman (1969), Main, 'Probate' (1975), Jones, *Wealth* (1980), Burchell, 'Opportunity' (1987), Bolton, 'Inequality' (1982), Soltow, *Men* (1975), Soltow, 'Inequality' (1979), Atack/Bateman, 'Egalitarianism' (1981), Newell, 'Inheritance' (1986),

Newell, 'Wealth' (1980), Herscovici, 'Distribution' (1993), Pope, 'Households' (1989), Gregson, 'Wealth' (1996), Ferrie, 'Wealth' (1994), Steckel, 'Poverty' (1990), Steckel/Moehling, 'Rising Inequality' (2001), Stewart, 'Migration' (2006), Clay/Jones, 'Riches' (2008), Walker, 'Opportunity' (2000), Canaday, 'Property' (2008), Stewart, 'Economic Opportunity' (2006).

12. Shanahan, 'Distribution' (1995) and Galt, 'Wealth' (1985) and McAloon, *Idle Rich* (2002). See also Rubinstein, 'Distribution' (1979). For a reference on the use of probate records in English economic history, see Owens et al. 'Measure' (2006). There are also nineteenth century studies of wealth inequality in South America. See Coatsworth (2008) and Johnson and Frank (2006).
13. For some recent examples, see Roine and Waldenström (2015), Nicolini and Palencia (2015, 2016), and Alfani (2015). See also Atkinson (2000) and Lindert (1986, 1991, 2000).
14. For Canada, Wolfson (1979) finds that adjustments to definitions of household or family size can have significant effects on measures of wealth distribution that vary by age in particularly understating the economic position of the elderly.
15. Shammas (1993: 421). A similar result has also been noted for Canada in Di Matteo (2016).
16. Australia, United Kingdom, France, United States, Switzerland, Finland, Norway, Denmark, Netherlands, Sweden.
17. Roine and Waldenström 2015: Figure 1).
18. See Morissette and Zhang (2006). For 1984, Morissette and Zhang report that in Canada by 1984, the top 10 percent owned 51.8 percent of wealth, while the next 40 percent owned 42.8 percent of wealth and the bottom 50 percent 5.4 percent. By 2005, they report that the share of the top 10 percent had grown to 58.2 percent while the next 40 had declined to 38.6 percent and that of the bottom 50 percent had dropped to 3.2 percent.
19. See Davies (1979), Wolfson (1979), and Oja (1983).
20. See Higgins and Williamson (2002) for a broader discussion.
21. While the share of the top 1 percent of income earners has grown, it remains substantially below the wealth share of the top 1 percent of wealth holders. For example, Statistics Canada reports that in 2013, Canada's top 1 percent of income earners earned 10.3 percent of income. See http://www.statcan.gc.ca/daily-quotidien/151103/dq151103a-eng.htm. The wealth share of the top 1 percent in 2005 was nearly 20 percent. For an overview of income distribution and its evolution in Canada and the United States, see Saez and Veall (2005). For an overview of wealth and income inequality trends for the United States and the world, see Wolff (2010) and Davies et al. (2011).

## References


Abad, L. A., & Junquera, P. A. (2017). Latin American Earnings Inequality in the Long Run. *Cliometrica, 11*(3), 349–374.

Alfani, G. (2015). Economic Inequality in Northwestern Italy: A Long-Term View (Fourteenth to Eighteenth Centuries). *Journal of Economic History, 75*(4), 1058–1096.

Alfani, G., & Ammannati, F. (2017). Long-Term Trends in Economic Inequality: The Case of the Florentine State, c. 1300–1800. *The Economic History Review, 70*(4), 1072–1102.

Alfani, G., & Ryckbosch, W. (2016). Growing Apart in Early Modern Europe? A Comparison of Inequality Trends in Italy and the Low Countries, 1500–1800. *Explorations in Economic History, 62*, 143–153.

Arrondel, L., & Grange, C. (2003). The Accumulation and Transmission of Wealth over Long Periods: Example of a Rural Family from Loire-Atlantique in the 19th and 20th Centuries. *The History of the Family: An International Quarterly, 2003*(8), 103–134.

Arrondel, L., & Grange, C. (2006). Transmission and Inequality of Wealth: An Empirical Study of Wealth Mobility from 1800 to 1938 in France. *Journal of Economic Inequality, 2006*(4), 209–232.

Arrondel, L., & Grange, C. (2014). Bequests and Family Traditions: The Case of Nineteenth Century France. *Review of Economics of the Household, 12*(3), 439–459.

Atack, J., & Bateman, F. (1981). Egalitarianism, Inequality, and Age: The Rural North in 1860. *Journal of Economic History, XLI*, 85–93.

Atkinson, A. B. (2000). Distribution of Income and Wealth in Britain over the Twentieth Century. In A. Halsey & J. Webb (Eds.), *Twentieth-Century British Social Trends*. Basingstoke: Palgrave Macmillan.

Atkinson, A. B. (2013, November). *Wealth and Inheritance in Britain from 1896 to the Present*. Centre for Analysis of Social Exclusion, No. 173.

Atkinson, A. B., & Harrison, A. (1978). *The Distribution of Personal Wealth in Britain*. Cambridge: Cambridge University Press.

Atkinson, A. B., Gordon, J. P. F., & Harrison, A. (1989). Trends in the Shares of Top Wealthholders in Britain: 1923–1989. *Oxford Bulletin of Economics and Statistics, 51*(3), 315–332.

Baskerville, P. (1999). Women and Investment in Late-Nineteenth-Urban Canada: Victoria and Hamilton, 1880–1901. *The Canadian Historical Review, 80*(2), 191–218.

Bolton, S. C. (1982). Inequality on the Southern Frontier: Arkansas County in the Arkansas Territory. *The Arkansas Historical Quarterly, 41*(1), 51–66.

Bouchard, G. (1998). Economic Inequalities in Saguenay Society, 1879–1949: A Descriptive Analysis. *The Canadian Historical Review, 79*(4), 660–690.

Burchell, R. A. (1987). Opportunity and the Frontier: Wealth-Holding in Twenty-Six Northern Californian Counties 1848–1880. *The Western Historical Quarterly, 18*(2), 177–196.

Canaday, N. (2008). The Accumulation of Property by Southern Blacks and Whites: Individual-Level Evidence from a South Carolina Cotton County, 1910–1919. *Explorations in Economic History, 45*, 51–75.

Clay, K., & Jones, R. (2008). Migrating to Riches? Evidence from the California Gold Rush. *The Journal of Economic History, 68*(4), 997–1027.

Coatsworth, J. H. (2008). Inequality, Institutions and Economic Growth in Latin America. *Journal of Latin American Studies, 40*(August), 545–569.

Darroch, G. (1983). Early Industrialization and Inequality in Toronto, 1861–1899. *Labour/Le Travailleur, 11*, 31–61.

Darroch, G., & Soltow, L. (1994). *Property and Inequality in Victorian Ontario Structural Patterns and Cultural Communities in the 1871 Census*. Toronto: University of Toronto Press.

Davies, J. B. (1979). On the Size Distribution of Wealth in Canada. *Review of Income and Wealth, 25*(3), 237–259.

Davies, J. B., & Shorrocks, A. F. (1999). The Distribution of Wealth. In A. B. Atkinson & F. Bourguignon (Eds.), *Handbook of Income Distribution* (Vol. 1). New York: Elsevier Science.

Davies, J., & Shorrocks, A. (2000). The Distribution of Wealth. In A. Atkinson & F. Bourguignon (Eds.), *Handbook of Income Distribution* (Vol. 1, pp. 605–675). North Holland, Amsterdam/New York: Elsevier.

Davies, J. B., Sandstrom, S., Shorrocks, A., & Wolff, E. N. (2011). The Level and Distribution of Global Household Wealth. *The Economic Journal, 121*, 223–254.

Di Matteo, L. (2016). Wealth Distribution and the Canadian Middle Class: Historical Evidence and Policy Implications. *Canadian Public Policy, 42*(2), 132–151.

Di Matteo, L., & George, P. (1992). Canadian Wealth Inequality in the Late Nineteenth Century: A Study of Wentworth County, Ontario, 1872–1902. *The Canadian Historical Review, LXXIII*, 453–483.

Di Matteo, L., & George, P. (1998). Patterns and Determinants of Wealth Among Probated Decedents in Wentworth County, Ontario, 1872–1902. *Histoire Sociale/Social History, XXXI*(61), 1–34.

Ferrie, J. (1994). The Wealth Accumulation of Antebellum European Immigrants to the U.S., 1840–1860. *Journal of Economic History, 54*, 1–33.

Fisher, J., Johnson, D., Smeeding, T., & Thompson, J. (2016a, September). *Inequality in 3D: Income, Consumption and Wealth. Washington Center for Equitable Growth* (Working paper series).

Fisher, J., Johnson, D., Latner, J. P., Smeeding, T., & Thompson, J. (2016b). Inequality and Mobility Using Income, Consumption, and Wealth for the

Same Individuals. *The Russell Sage Foundation Journal of the Social Sciences, 2*, 44–58.

Gallman, R. E. (1969). Trends in the Size Distribution of Wealth in the Nineteenth Century: Some Speculations. In L. Soltow (Ed.), *Six Papers on the Size Distribution of Wealth and Income*. New York: National Bureau of Economic Research.

Galt, M. N. (1985). Wealth and Income in New Zealand 1870 to 1939. Unpublished PhD Thesis, Victoria University, Wellington

Gregson, M. E. (1996). Wealth Accumulation and Distribution in the Midwest in the Late Nineteenth Century. *Explorations in Economic History, 33*, 524–538.

Gwyn, J., & Siddiq, F. K. (1992). Wealth Distribution in Nova Scotia During the Confederation Era, 1851 and 1871. *The Canadian Historical Review, LXXIII*(4), 435–452.

Hamilton, G. C., Keay, I., & Lewis, F. (2017). Contributions to Canadian Economic History: The Last 30 Years. *Canadian Journal of Economics, 50*(5), 1632–1657.

Herscovici, S. (1993). The Distribution of Wealth in Nineteenth Century Boston: Inequality Among Natives and Immigrants, 1860. *Explorations in Economic History, 30*, 321–335.

Higgins, M., & Williamson, J. G. (2002). Explaining Inequality the World Round: Cohort Size, Kuznets Curves, and Openness. *Southeast Asian Studies, 40*(3), 268–302. Reprinted in B. Milanovic (Ed.) (2012). *Globalization and Inequality*. Cheltenham: Elgar.

Johnson, L. L., & Frank, Z. (2006). Cities and Wealth in the South Atlantic: Buenos Aires and Rio de Janeiro Before 1860. *Comparative Studies in Society and History, 48*(3), 634–668.

Jones, A. H. (1980). *Wealth of A Nation to Be: The American Colonies on the Eve of the Revolution*. New York: Columbia Press.

Krueger, D., & Perri, F. (2006). Does Income Inequality Lead to Consumption Equality? Evidence and Theory. *Review of Economic Studies, 73*(1), 163–193.

Kuznets, S. (1955). Economic Growth and Income Inequality. *American Economic Review, XLV*(1), 1–28.

Kuznets, S. (1966). *Modern Economic Growth Rate, Structure and Spread*. New Haven: Yale University Press.

Lindert, P. H. (1986). Unequal English Wealth Since 1670. *The Journal of Political Economy, 94*(6), 1127–1162.

Lindert, P. H. (1991). Toward a Comparative History of Income and Wealth. In Y. S. Brenner, H. Kaelble, & M. Thomas (Eds.), *Income Distribution in Historical Perspective* (pp. 212–231). Cambridge: Cambridge University Press.

Lindert, P. H. (2000). Three Centuries of Inequality in Britain and America. In A. B. Atkinson & F. Bourguignon (Eds.), *Handbook of Income Distribution* (Vol. 1). Amsterdam: North-Holland.

Lindert, P. H., & Williamson, J. G. (1985). Growth, Equality and History. *Explorations in Economic History, 22*, 341–377.
Lindert, P. H., & Williamson, J. G. (2012). *American Incomes 1774–1860.* National Bureau of Economic Research, Working Paper 18396.
Lindert, P. H., & Williamson, J. G. (2016). *Unequal Gains: American Growth and Inequality Since 1700.* Princeton: Princeton University Press.
Main, G. L. (1975). Probate Records as a Source for Early American History. *William and Mary Quarterly, 32*(1), 89–99. 3rd ser.
Malinowski, M., & van Zanden, J. L. (2016). Income and Its Distribution in Preindustrial Poland. *Cliometrica.* https://doi.org/10.1007/s11698-016-0154-5.
McAloon, J. (2002). *No Idle Rich: The Wealthy in Canterbury and Otago 1840–1914.* Dunedin: University of Otago Press.
Meyer, B. D., & Sullivan, J. X. (2017, August). *Consumption and Income Inequality in the U.S. Since the 1960s.* NBER Working Paper No. 23655.
Milanovic, B. (2016). *Global Inequality: A New Approach for the Age of Globalisation.* Cambridge, MA: Harvard University Press.
Morissette, R., & Zhang, X. (2006). *Revisiting Wealth Inequality.* Perspectives. Statistics Canada No. 75-001-XIE, pp. 5–16.
Newell, W. H. (1980). The Wealth of Testators and Its Distribution: Butler County Ohio, 1803–65. In J. D. Smith (Ed.), *Modelling the Distribution and Intergenerational Transmission of Wealth, NBER Studies in Income and Wealth* (Vol. 46, pp. 95–138). Chicago: University of Chicago Press.
Newell, W. H. (1986). Inheritance on the Maturing Frontier: Butler County Ohio, 1803–1865. In S. L. Engerman & R. E. Gallman (Eds.), *Long-Term Factors in American Economic Growth, NBER Studies in Income and Wealth* (Vol. 51, pp. 261–303). Chicago: University of Chicago Press.
Nicolini, E. A., & Palencia, F. R. (2015). *Comparing Income and Wealth Inequality in Pre-Industrial Economies. Lessons from Spain in the 18th Century.* http://www.academia.edu/1752082/Comparing_Income_and_Wealth_Inequality_in_Pre-Industrial_economies._Lessons_from_Spain_in_the_18th_century
Nicolini, E. A., & Palencia, F. R. (2016). Decomposing Income Inequality in a Backward Pre-Industrial Economy: Old Castile (Spain) in the Middle of the Eighteenth Century. *The Economic History Review, 69*(3), 747–772.
Ohlsson, H., Roine, J., & Waldenström, D. (2008). Long-Run Changes in the Concentration of Wealth: An Overview of Recent Findings. In J. B. Davies (Ed.), *Personal Wealth from a Global Perspective.* Oxford: Oxford University Press.
Oja, G. (1983). The Distribution of Wealth in Canada. *Review of Income and Wealth, 29*(2), 161–173.
Osberg, L., & Siddiq, F. K. (1993). The Acquisition of Wealth in Nova Scotia in the Late Nineteenth Century. *Research in Economic Inequality, 4*, 181–202.

Owens, A., Green, D.R., Bailey, C. and Kay, A.C. (2006). A Measure of Worth: Probate Valuations, Personal Wealth and Indebtedness in England, 1810–40. *Historical Research, 79*(205), 383–403.

Piketty, T. (2014). *Capital in the 21st Century*. Cambridge, MA: Harvard University Press.

Pope, C. L. (1989). Households on the American Frontier: The Distribution of Income and Wealth in Utah 1850–1900. In D. W. Galenson (Ed.), *Markets in History: Economic Studies of the Past* (pp. 148–189). Cambridge: Cambridge University Press.

Reeves, R. V. (2017). *Dream Hoarders. How the American Upper Middle Class Is Leaving Everyone Else in the Dust*. Washington, DC: Brooking.

Reis, J. (2016). Deviant Behaviour? Inequality in Portugal 1565–1770. *Cliometrica*. https://doi.org/10.1007/s11698-016-0152-7.

Roine, J., & Waldenström, D. (2015). Long-Run Trends in the Distribution of Income and Wealth. In A. B. Atkinson & F. Bourguignon (Eds.), *Handbook of Income Distribution* (Vol. 2A, pp. 469–592). Amsterdam: Elsevier.

Rubinstein, W. D. (1979). The Distribution of Personal Wealth in Victoria 1860–1974. *Australian Economic History Review, 19*, 26–41.

Saez, E., & Veall, M. (2005). The Evolution of High Incomes in Northern America: Lessons from Canadian Evidence. *American Economic Review, 95*, 831–849.

Shammas, C. (1993). A New Look at Long-Term Trends in Wealth Inequality in the United States. *The American Historical Review, 98*(2), 412–431.

Shanahan, M. P. (1995). The Distribution of Personal Wealth in South Australia, 1905–1915. *Australian Economic History Review, 35*(2), 82–111.

Siddiq, F. K. (1988). The Size Distribution of Probate Wealth-Holdings in Nova Scotia in the Late 19th Century. *Acadiensis, 18*(1), 136–147.

Siddiq, F. K., & Gwyn, J. (1991). The Importance of Probate Inventories in Estimating the Distribution of Wealth. *Nova Scotia Historical Review, 11*, 103–117.

Soltow, L. (1975). *Men and Wealth in the United States 1850–1870*. New Haven: Yale University Press.

Soltow, L. (1979). Inequality Amidst Abundance: Land Ownership in Early 19th Century Ohio. *Ohio History, 88*(2), 133–151.

Soltow, L. (1981). The Distribution of Property Values in England and Wales in 1798. *The Economic History Review, 34*(2), 60–70.

Soltow, L. (1989). *Distribution of Wealth and Income in the United States in 1798*. Pittsburgh: University of Pittsburgh Press.

Steckel, R. H. (1990). Poverty and Prosperity: A Longitudinal Study of Wealth Accumulation, 1850–1860. *The Review of Economics and Statistics, 72*(2), 275–285.

Steckel, R. H., & Moehling, C. M. (2001). Rising Inequality: Trends in the Distribution of Wealth in Industrializing New England. *Journal of Economic History, 61*, 160–183.

Stewart, J. I. (2006). Migration to the Agricultural Frontier and Wealth Accumulation, 1860–1870. *Explorations in Economic History, 43*(4), 547–577.

Walker, T. R. (2000). Economic Opportunity on the Urban Frontier: Wealth and Nativity in Early San Francisco. *Explorations in Economic History, 37*, 258–277.

Williamson, J. G., & Lindert, P. H. (1980). *American Inequality: A Macroeconomic History*. New York: Academic Press.

Wolff, E. N. (2010, March). *Recent Trends in household Wealth in the United States: Rising Debt and the Middle Class Squeeze-an Update to 2007*. Levy Economics Institute. Working Paper No. 589.

Wolff, E. N., & Marley, M. (1989). Long-Term Trends in U.S. Wealth Inequality: Methodological Issues and Results. In R. E. Lipsey & H. S. Tice (Eds.), *The Measurement of Saving and Wealth*. Chicago: NBER.

Wolfson, M. C. (1979). Wealth and the Distribution of Income, Canada 1969–70. *The Review of Income and Wealth, 25*(2), 129–140.

CHAPTER 3

# Wealth Inequality: Facts, Figures and Approaches to Its Study

**Abstract** Methodological issues include defining wealth, units of observation, biases of the data source, asset coverage, sampling, and institutional differences. Sources include survey data, estate tax data, probate, census, and income tax data. The Canadian wealth inequality figures are for 1851–2012 and come from probate records, published scholarly estimates, Statistics Canada Survey data, and federal estate tax data. The US wealth inequality estimates are for 1680–2012 and come from secondary sources using probate, census, survey, and tax data. Estimates for the United Kingdom come from primary and secondary sources for the years from 1668 to 2013, including probate and estate tax data. Inequality measures used are the Gini coefficient and the top 1 and 10 percent wealth shares.

**Keywords** Probate • Estate tax • Gini • Top 1 percent

## 3.1 Inequality Data

Compiling long-term statistics on wealth and wealth inequality is crucial to the efforts needed for understanding the long-term trends and determinants of wealth distribution, but doing so is also a very challenging endeavor. There are potentially several methodological issues when it comes to examining wealth inequality that may be compounded when



L. Di Matteo, *The Evolution and Determinants of Wealth Inequality in the North Atlantic Anglo-Sphere, 1668–2013*,
https://doi.org/10.1007/978-3-319-89773-8_3

international comparisons over time are made. Among them are the actual definition of what wealth is, the units of observation, assorted biases of the data source being made use of, asset inclusion and coverage, sampling differences, as well as institutional differences when data from different countries are compared.[1]

It is well known that survey data, estate tax data, and income tax data (the main sources used in the literature) all face some limitations in their ability to accurately capture wealth (especially with respect to observations near the top of the wealth distribution) and can therefore sometimes paint very different pictures. For example, Bricker et al. (2016) note for the United States that top share estimates derived from administrative income tax data generally overstate income and wealth concentration levels relative to household Survey of Consumer Finance data.

These issues are exacerbated when long-term international comparisons of historical wealth inequality are to be made given the diversity of data sources over time as well as differences in national standards of data collection and coverage. Roine and Waldenström (2015) in their look at long-term trends in wealth inequality use international data sets that cover households, adults, families, and males only, and that were generated from surveys, tax records, and probate. They note that even when a common unit of comparison is available across countries (e.g., households), the definition is not identical across countries and can even vary over time within a country.

Reed (2014) suggests that making international comparisons of wealth inequality can be exceptionally challenging, and unless steps are taken to ensure that data collection is proceeding under consistent methodologies, one may be simply measuring differences in wealth data collection rather than any underlying differences in the distribution of wealth between countries. Indeed, recent research has tried to combine and reconcile various data sources such as survey data and named lists (Vermuelen 2016), estate tax and income tax data (Garbinti et al. 2016), survey data and income tax data (Bricker et al. 2016), and income tax data and estate tax data (Saez and Zucman 2016).

Nevertheless, the ultimate constraint is having any data at all to measure, and as Roine and Waldenström (2015: 5) write, sometimes more is required than simply being able to select and estimate an appropriate inequality measure and that indeed 'when it comes to the study of long run inequality the availability of any data at all is often the binding constraint.' While ideally one should try and reconcile alternate data sources in some matter, in actual practice, this can be difficult using international data that spans both time and space.

For example, probate wealth data often marks studies from the more distant past when inequality was presumably higher, while survey or tax wealth data marks more modern periods when inequality is believed to have declined. At the same time, probate data can be biased toward those of higher socioeconomic status, and therefore the wealth distribution estimates omit those at the bottom of the distribution making the resulting numbers seem more equitable. As for combining different sources into a consistent estimate, this may be feasible over a period of historical time for a given national or geographic region but is difficult for international comparisons.[2]

In light of these issues, the approach in this paper will be to use the numerous estimates made over time obtained from a variety of sources to provide a range of inequality estimates both at points in time, over time, and within the countries being examined. It should be noted that the definition of wealth as well as the underlying units for comparison differ across these countries both at points in time and over time. Units of study range from individuals to families to households, while the definition of wealth includes gross estate, estimates of net worth, and household wealth.

As a result, non-parametric data smoothing procedures—local polynomial smoothing and locally weighted scatter plot smoothing (LOWESS)—will be used in an effort to deal with the invariable outliers generated by different data sources. Determining longer-term trends in inequality over time requires an estimation technique that is not going to be as sensitive to outliers in the data. Non-parametric estimation is a flexible curve fitting technique that operates as a form of data smoothing or local averaging rather than a pre-specified or parametric relationship which can impose a preordained functional form requiring assumptions about the parameters and data, such as normality or large sample sizes.

Non-parametric smoothing techniques provide a versatile method for minimizing the impact of outliers without reference to a specified parametric model and also help to bridge gaps of missing data between adjacent data points, which is often the case for historical wealth data.[3] In the absence of reconciliation across different data sources spanning both time and geographic space, non-parametric regression provides a potential if imperfect method for accommodating what is inevitably a diversity of data differences. However, a potential disadvantage of non-parametric techniques is the greater computational intensity for the estimation methods used.

## 3.2 Canada

The wealth inequality estimates obtained and presented here for Canada are for the period 1851–2012 and come from four main sources: (1) historical wealth micro-data collected from probate records, (2) previously published scholarly estimates, (3) Statistics Canada Survey data, and (4) Federal Government estate tax data. Some elaboration particularly with respect to the historical probate wealth micro-data is in order, given that it forms the basis for most of the Canadian wealth inequality estimates for the period prior to 1930.

The historical probate wealth micro-data was collected for four regional data sets: they are Wentworth County, Ontario (1872–1927), Thunder Bay District, Ontario (1885–1927), Ontario (1892, 1902), and Manitoba (1875–1927). These data sets vary in size with Ontario 1892 and 1902 consisting of 3515 and 3641 individuals, Wentworth County at 2516, Thunder Bay District at 2338, and Manitoba at 826.[4]

The primary data source is the probate records of Ontario and Manitoba Surrogate Courts, with probate being an institutional process that transferred property from the dead to the living and as part of the process did a detailed market based evaluation of assets. Probate inventories provided detailed valuations of estates with the wealth recorded in a number of categories, including household goods and furniture, stock in trade, livestock, life insurance, stocks and shares, securities, cash on hand and in bank, book debts, promissory notes, and mortgages and real estate.[5]

There have been several separate wealth inequality studies done for Canada for the nineteenth century, and these studies have invariably included estimates of inequality in terms of either Gini coefficients[6] or wealth shares by decile. In a series of papers, Siddiq (1988) and Gwyn and Siddiq (1992) looked at the distribution of wealth in Nova Scotia using probate records and provide estimates of Gini Coefficients and wealth shares for 1851 and 1871. Darroch (1983) uses municipal property assessment rolls and analyzes inequality of real estate holdings for Toronto for the period 1861–1899, again providing some wealth share and Gini coefficient estimates.

Moving into the twentieth century, there are a number of wealth and financial asset surveys by Statistics Canada, which have provided data for estimates of wealth distribution. Public use micro-data are available from Statistics Canada with the Survey of Consumer Finances and the Survey of Financial Security. For 1970 and 1977, estimates of wealth inequality are taken from Oja (1987), while Gini Coefficients and wealth shares were calculated from micro-data files for 1984, 1999, 2005, and 2012.[7] The Statistics Canada micro-data includes estimates of family net worth along with numerous individual and family characteristics as well as detail on specific assets.[8]

While estimates of Canadian wealth inequality for this paper are available at various points in time for the period 1851–1927 and 1970–2012, there is a large gap for the period 1927–1969. In an effort to obtain some estimates of wealth inequality for this critical period spanning the Great Depression as well as World War II and the post-war era, aggregate federal government estate taxation information was used to construct wealth inequality measures for the years 1950–1952 and 1959–1960.

Estate and gift taxes have a long history in Canada at both the federal and provincial levels.[9] Provincial succession duties—that is, a tax on the beneficiary in respect of the amount received from an estate—were levied in numerous provinces in the 1890s and remained in effect in most provinces until the 1970s.[10] The Federal government imposed estate taxes—a duty imposed on the value of property passing at the time of death—in 1941, under the Succession Duty Act that was then replaced by the Estate Tax Act in 1959.[11] While the differences in practice between these two acts were minor in terms of the actual application and administration of estate taxes, in terms of reporting, prior to 1959, the Taxation Statistics reports estate income on which taxation was levied, while after 1959 estate size and tax on the taxable value are reported.

The Estate Tax was repealed in 1972 as part of a process of Canadian tax reform. While generally a minor source of Canadian federal government revenue, Bird (1978) argues that the abolition of the federal estate tax was the most important tax reform of the post-World War II era in that it symbolized a retreat from direct attempts to affect the distribution of Canadian wealth via taxation. Bird (1978: 144) concluded that the move away from estate taxation generated few benefits for Canada and that it 'has paid a significant price in terms of reduced equality of opportunity, probably increased inequality of wealth, and certainly increased fossilization of the structure of wealth'.[12]

Department of National Revenue, Taxation Statistics for the years 1952, 1953, and 1954 were used to estimate the distribution of the income from estates for the years 1950–1952 as a proxy for the wealth distribution, while those for 1961 and 1962 were used to estimate the distribution of estates for 1959 (1959–1960) and 1960 (1960–1961).[13]

There were 3990 estates in 1950, 4610 in 1951, and 5500 in 1952. The income per estate by income class was calculated, and then based on the number of estates in each income class, a simulated distribution was constructed with the individuals in each income class assigned the average estate income for that class. It should be noted that the resulting estimates for distribution were not age-sex adjusted.[14]

This process was repeated for 1959 and 1960 but with some modification, given that there was an exemption for estates under $50,000 in size resulting in an absence of these estates in the Taxation Statistics Tables. Using the numbers of estates by estate size ranges provided in the tables, an exponential function was used to interpolate the numbers of estates below $50,000 and the average estate value used was the average of the range employed. With this adjustment, there were a total of 4092 estates in 1959 and 7128 in 1960, and these were used to construct a simulated wealth distribution with the individuals in each estate size class assigned the average estate size for that class. Detailed tables illustrating this estate tax inequality data for 1950–1952 and 1959–1960 are provided in Appendix 1.[15] All the Canadian data used in this analysis is provided in Appendix 2.

## 3.3 United States

The wealth inequality estimates for the United States come from an assortment of secondary sources and research, and span the period 1680–2012. It should be noted that they are for varying levels of aggregation as they include wealth inequality estimates calculated for the entire country as well as for separate states, regions, as well as some urban areas resulting in considerable geographic diversity for these point estimates. Moreover, there is some variation as to whether decile shares or Gini coefficients are consistently available over time. Appendix 3 provides the compiled United States wealth inequality data used in this paper.

Roine and Waldenström (2014, 2015) provide a convenient set of wealth shares for the period 1774–2010 for the top 1, 5, and 10 percent, which they also take from a substantial body of secondary literature. Their work uses estimates from Shammas (1993), Kopczuk and Saez (2004), Lindert (2000), Wolff (1987, 1996), and Kennickell (2009, 2011). Piketty (2014) also provides wealth decile and top 1 percent shares based on the work of Kennickell (2009, 2011) and Wolff (1994).

Soltow (1989) presents Gini coefficients for the nineteenth-century United States, estimated from census data as well as includes other estimates done by other scholars for the Charleston District in South Carolina, New Jersey, and Suffolk County, Massachusetts, for the period from 1720 to 1983. Jones (1980) presents estimates of Gini coefficients and wealth shares for the 13 colonies on the eve of the American Revolution constructed from colonial probate data.

Shammas (1993) provides wealth inequality estimates for the period 1774–1986, incorporating work by Lindert and Williamson, and Jones as well as household net worth data from survey data. Gallman (1969) provides decile shares of US personal wealth from the US manuscript census for the period 1810–1900. Osberg (1984) includes estimates done for 1962 and 1973 from US survey data.

Finally, some late twentieth century numbers are produced by Pfeffer et al. (2013) spanning the years from 1984 to 2011 as well as by Davies et al. (2011) for 2000. Pfeffer et al. provide Gini coefficients for US net worth data from the U.S. Panel Survey of Income Dynamics, while Davies et al. provide an estimate of the Gini coefficient of inequality for household wealth from Survey of Consumer Finance data. In addition, wealth inequality estimates for the United States by Saez and Zucman (2016) constructed for the period 1913–2012 using capitalized income tax data are also included in this data set, as are some estimates from the Chartbook of Economic Inequality.[16]

These estimates of US wealth inequality are quite diverse, combining census, probate, tax, and survey data, but also different units of observation including households and families as well as for the case of the nineteenth century free households or free adults as well as some for adult males only. In addition, there are some gap periods in the US data also. In the case of Gini coefficients, there is an absence of Gini coefficient estimates in this data set from 1870 to the late 1950s. There is fortunately more comprehensive coverage to the data when it comes to the wealth share of the top 1 and 10 percent for this period. The presence of data gaps for either one measure or another make it especially valuable to have more than one measure of wealth inequality when trying to ascertain the evolution of long-term trends.

Another important dimension with respect to any discussion of American wealth inequality is again the effects and importance of estate taxation. While estate taxes in various forms have a long history in the United States—as far back as the post-revolutionary period—the modern estate tax system begins in 1916 via the passing of the Revenue Act.[17] The Revenue Act of 1916 was enacted in response to the financial needs of World War I and at that time carried a $50,000 estate exemption and saw rates ranging from 1 to 10 percent. Like Canada, these taxes made up a relatively small share of total federal revenues accounting for at the most 1 to 2 percent.[18] In terms of maximum rates, they rose dramatically from 1920 to 1940, were at a peak from 1940 to the mid-1970s, and then began to drop.[19]

In 1976, there was a major overhaul of the system when the Tax Reform Act (TRA) was passed, which combined the previously separate exemptions for estate and gift taxes into a single unified tax and saw a reduction in the top rates from 77 percent down to 55 percent by 1981.[20] In the period since 1977, less than 2 percent of deceased adults have left estates large enough to be taxable and at present a relatively small percentage of estates are taxable. The Economic Growth and Tax Relief Reconciliation Act of 2001 began eliminating the death tax with a scheduled phase-out of rates, but as a result of sunset provisions in 2011, the estate tax reverted to the 1997 law with a top rate of 55 percent.[21] While the Trump tax reforms scheduled to take effect in 2018 vowed to eliminate the US federal estate tax, the estate tax has been retained, but the exemption amount has been raised substantially.[22]

## 3.4 United Kingdom

The wealth inequality estimates for the United Kingdom come from primary and secondary sources that span the years from 1668 to 2013. They are essentially national estimates though the definition of nation varies with United Kingdom and England and Wales both being used in this chapter somewhat interchangeably. As with Canada and the United States, the aim was to collect as many estimates as possible for Gini coefficients and wealth shares of the top 1 and 10 percent with these estimates provided in Appendix 4.

A key data source is the net estate values from probate estate data for England and Wales, compiled by Peter Lindert,[23] for the period stretching from 1661 to 1875. This data set contains 12,592 individual observations and was used to calculate Gini coefficients and the wealth share of the top 1 and 10 percent for selected years starting in 1668 and ending in 1875.[24] Roine and Waldenström (2014, 2015) provide a series for the wealth share of the top 10 percent, stretching from 1740 to 2005. Davies and Shorrocks (2000: 641) provide estimates of both a Gini coefficient and the top decile share for UK adjusted net worth for the years 1966, 1976, 1985, and 1993. Similar numbers are provided in a website publication by the Institute for Economic Affairs publication for the years 2006, 2008, and 2010.[25]

Rowlingson (2012) provides estates of both top decile shares and Gini coefficients for wealth for select years from 1976 to 2005. The study of Di Matteo et al. (2012) is the source for Gini coefficient estates for probate wealth for 1870 and 1902, while Davies et al. (2011) provide a Gini coefficient estimate for household wealth in 2000. Piketty's estimates for the United Kingdom for the wealth share of the top 1 and 10 percent for selected years over the period 1810–2010 are also used.[26] Finally, recent estimates of wealth shares constructed by Alvaredo et al. (2017) for the top 1 and 10 percent from 1895 to 2013, constructed from estate data, are also used, as well as estimates from the Chartbook of Economic Inequality.[27]

While England also has a long history of probate and succession duties stretching back to a stamp duty enacted on probated wills in 1694, the modern United Kingdom system of estate taxation as a tax on property passing on death with higher rates begins in 1894. The Finance Act of 1894 replaced probate duties and other estate fees then in existence, and when introduced, approximately 15 percent of estates were liable for tax, but the proportion began to rise—given the fixed 100-pound exemption threshold—until 40 percent of estates were liable to tax by 1945. The threshold was then increased to 2000 pounds and the proportion liable to tax fell to 10 percent, and there was a downward trend in the proportion liable to taxation from this until the 1990s.[28]

The estate duty tax was replaced in 1975 by a Capital Transfer Tax that was then renamed the Inheritance Tax in 1986.[29] It was accompanied by declining rates starting in 1981 that reduced the rate on transfers at death to 60 percent from 75 percent. Moreover, in 1986, reforms were made that allowed donors to escape the tax by making gifts that they survived by seven years. By 2009, the rate had fallen to 40 percent on the value of estates over a basic threshold.[30] However, starting in the 2017/2018 taxation year, the threshold amounts at which taxation applies will be raised and is expected to continue increasing until 2020/2021.[31]

## Notes

1. Wolff (1991: 94).
2. For example, Garbinti et al. (2016) combine income tax data, inheritance registers, national accounts, and wealth surveys to deliver consistent and unified wealth distributions, but they do so only for France from 1800 to 2014.
3. For a discussion, see Hardle (1991: 3–13). See also Cleveland (1979, 1985, 1993).
4. These data sets were collected with financial assistance via three standard research grants provided by the Social Sciences and Humanities Research Council of Canada over the periods 1991–1994, 1999–2002, and 2007–2010.
5. Probate data is potentially subject to a number of biases. Probated decedents were generally of higher socioeconomic status and estate taxes may have provided some incentives for estate administrators to underestimate assets. Ontario and Manitoba both brought in succession duties in the 1890s, but the exemptions were broad enough to provide little incentive to underestimate estate values. For some additional details on probate as a source of wealth data, these data sets, their construction, and previous use, see Di Matteo (1997, 1998, 2004, 2012, 2013a, 2016a, b).
6. A Gini coefficient is an inequality measure that takes on a value between zero and 1 with 0 denoting complete equality and 1 complete inequality. There is increasing inequality in a society as its Gini coefficients estimates increase toward 1. For a discussion of Gini coefficients and other inequality measures, see Cowell (2009).
7. These sources are as follows: Statistics Canada. Household Surveys Division, Statistics Canada Survey of Consumer Finances, 1977 [Canada]: Economic Family and Unattached Individuals Income, Assets and Debts Study Documentation, October 7, 2015; Statistics Canada. Household Surveys Division. Survey of Consumer Finances, 1984 [Canada]: Economic Family and Unattached Individuals Income, Assets, Debt. Study Documentation. October 7, 2015; Income Statistics Division, Statistics Canada.

   Survey of Financial Security, 1999 [Canada]: Economic Family File Study Documentation October 7, 2015; Income Statistics Division, Statistics Canada.

   Survey of Financial Security, 2005 [Canada] Study Documentation, October 7, 2015; Income Statistics Division, Statistics Canada Survey of Financial Security, 2012 [Canada] Study Documentation October 7, 2015.

8. These include deposits, savings bonds, cash on hand, registered retirement savings plans, registered home ownership plans, other liquid and non-liquid assets, value of vehicles owned, the value of owner occupied homes, and vacation homes.
9. Goodman (1995).
10. See Perry (1984: 125).
11. By the 1960s, the Federal Estate Tax for domiciled decedents allowed a basic exemption of $40,000, with additional exemptions if there were surviving spouses and children. Rates of taxation ranged from 10 to 16 percent for the first $20,000 of taxable estate value. For values of $20,000 to $200,000, the tax rate ranged from 18 to 26 percent. From $200,000 to $750,000, the rates ranged from 28 to 42 percent. From $750,000 to $1,800,000, the rates continued rising eventually reaching 52 percent. On remaining amounts, the rate was 54 percent. See Department of National Revenue, Taxation Division, Taxation Statistics 1964, Queen's Printer, Ottawa, Canada, pp. 80–81. There was also a Gift Tax first imposed in 1935. See Perry (1984: 228). By the 1960s, the Gift Tax ranged from 10 percent on an aggregate taxable gift value of $5000 and under to 28 percent on amounts over $1,000,000. The Federal Gift Tax was also repealed in 1972. See Canada Year Book, 1962, p. 1021. For a survey of post-war Canadian fiscal and tax history, see Perry (1989).
12. Bird (1978: 140) also notes a report of the Ontario Government's Taxation Committee in 1967 that notes that wealth taxation and death taxes in particular had a significant role in controlling extremes of wealth.
13. Data sources: 1950, Estates (Table J, p. 119), Department of National Revenue, Taxation Division, Taxation Statistics 1952, Queen's Printer, Ottawa, Canada; 1951, Estates (Table 10, p. 71), Department of National Revenue, Taxation Division, Taxation Statistics 1953, Queen's Printer, Ottawa, Canada; 1952, Estates (Table 10, p. 70), Department of National Revenue, Taxation Division, Taxation Statistics 1955, Queen's Printer, Ottawa, Canada; 1959–1960, Table 2, Estate Tax Department of National Revenue, Taxation Division, Taxation Statistics 1961, Queen's Printer, Ottawa, Canada; 1960–1961, Table 2, Estate Tax Department of National Revenue, Taxation Division, Taxation Statistics 1962, Queen's Printer, Ottawa, Canada.
14. Distribution of these estates by age categories was not available in these tables, and therefore estate multiplier estimates were not possible. It should be noted that work in progress by Davies and Di Matteo (2017) is constructing wealth distribution estimates using the estate multiplier for the top 1 percent using more detailed Canadian federal estate tax data, and the preliminary results have generated inequality estimates somewhat higher than the ones generated here.

15. It should again be noted that the wealth inequality estimates done here are not in any way adjusted for social class or mortality. As a result, the inequality estimates here show somewhat greater equality in the wealth distribution than would be the case if there was such adjustments.
16. Accessed January 2016. https://www.chartbookofeconomicinequality.com/
17. US federal taxes on wealth at death have been enacted since 1797, often in response to revenue needs in time of war or crisis. For example, they were enacted to cover expenses in both the US Civil War and the Spanish-American War and then repealed.
18. Congressional Budget Office (2009: 1).
19. DeLong (2003: Figure 4).
20. Changes in 1981 came with the passage of the Economic Recovery Tax Act (ERTA) that expanded marital deductions.
21. The Economic Growth and Tax Relief Reconciliation Act of 2001 (EGTRRA) phased out the estate tax beginning in 2001, essentially by increasing the tax exempt amount of an estate and by reducing the top marginal tax rate an estate. In 2010, the estate tax was temporarily repealed. Starting in 2011, the estate tax is reinstated, with an effective exemption amount of $1 million and a maximum marginal tax rate of 55 percent. See Congressional Budget Office (2009). For a longer-term history of US Federal estate taxation, see also Johnson and Eller (1998). As well, the American Taxpayer Relief Act (ATRA) of 2012 made the reversion permanent and included a five million dollar exemption indexed for inflation as well as top rates of 40 percent.
22. https://www.forbes.com/sites/ashleaebeling/2017/12/21/final-tax-bill-includes-huge-estate-tax-win-for-the-rich-the-22-4-million-exemption/#482eb4801d54
23. See Lindert (1986).
24. The years used are: 1668, 1669, 1670, 1698, 1699, 1700, 1729, 1730, 1731, 1738, 1739, 1740, 1741, 1810, and 1875.
25. Wealth Inequality the Facts. Institute for Economic Affairs. http://www.iea.org.uk/sites/default/files/publications/files/Wealth%20inequality%20briefing%20formatted.pdf
26. Piketty (2014) Figure 10.5.
27. Accessed January 2016. https://www.chartbookofeconomicinequality.com/
28. Atkinson (2013: 8).
29. Atkinson (2013: 7).
30. Boadway et al. (2009).
31. See http://www.telegraph.co.uk/financial-services/investments/inheritance-tax/inheritance-tax-changes/

## References

Alvaredo, F., Atkinson, A. B., & Morelli, S. (2017, January). *Top Wealth Shares in the UK over More than a Century.* Centre for Studies in Economics and Finance, Working Paper No. 464.

Atkinson, A. B. (2013, November). *Wealth and Inheritance in Britain from 1896 to the Present.* Centre for Analysis of Social Exclusion, No. 173.

Bird, R. (1978). Canada's Vanishing Death Taxes. *Osgoode Hall Law Journal, 16*(1), 133–145.

Boadway, R., Chamberlain, E., & Emmerson, C. (2009). *Taxation of Wealth and Wealth Transfers: Appendices.* Prepared for the Report of a commission on Reforming the Tax System for the 21st Century, Chaired by Sir James Mirrlees, The Institute for Fiscal Studies. www.ofs.org.uk/mirrleesreview

Bricker, J., Henriques, A., Krimmel, J., & Sabelhaus, J. (2016). Estimating Top Income and Wealth Shares: Sensitivity to Data and Methods. *American Economic Review: Papers and Proceedings, 106*(5), 641–645.

Cleveland, W. S. (1979). Robust Locally Weighted Regression and Smoothing Scatterplots. *Journal of the American Statistical Association, 74*, 829–836.

Cleveland, W. S. (1985). *The Elements of Graphing.* Monterey: Wadsworth.

Cleveland, W. S. (1993). *Visualizing Data.* Summit: Hobart.

Congression Budget Office. (2009, December 18). *Federal Estate and Gift Taxes.* Economic and Business Issue Brief.

Cowell, F. A. (2009, December). Measuring Inequality. http://darp.lse.ac.uk/papersDB/Cowell_measuringinequality3.pdf

Darroch, G. (1983). Early Industrialization and Inequality in Toronto, 1861–1899. *Labour/Le Travailleur, 11*, 31–61.

Davies, J. B., & Di Matteo, L. (2017). *Filling the Gap: Examining Canadian Wealth Inequality Over the Long Run.* Paper Prepared for Presentation at the 51st Annual Meetings of the Canadian Economic Association, Antigonish, Nova Scotia. Manuscript.

Davies, J., & Shorrocks, A. (2000). The Distribution of Wealth. In A. Atkinson & F. Bourguignon (Eds.), *Handbook of Income Distribution* (Vol. 1, pp. 605–675). North Holland, Amsterdam/New York: Elsevier.

Davies, J. B., Sandstrom, S., Shorrocks, A., & Wolff, E. N. (2011). The Level and Distribution of Global Household Wealth. *The Economic Journal, 121*, 223–254.

Delong, B. (2003). Bequests: An Historical Perspective, Chapter 2. In A. H. Munnell & A. Sundén (Eds.), *Death and Sollars: The Role of Gifts and Bequests in America.* Washington, DC: Brookings Institution Press.

Di Matteo, L. (1997). The Determinants of Wealth and Asset Holding in Nineteenth Century Canada: Evidence from Micro-data. *Journal of Economic History, 57*(4), 907–934.

Di Matteo, L. (1998). Wealth Accumulation and the Life-Cycle in Economic History: Implications of Alternative Approaches to Data. *Explorations in Economic History, 35*(3), 296–324. *Erratum, 36*(1), 107.

Di Matteo, L. (2004). Resource Boom and Bust, 1885–1920: Regional Wealth Evidence from Probate Records. *Australian Economic History Review, 44*(1), 52–78.

Di Matteo, L. (2012). Land and Inequality in Canada 1870–1930. *Scandinavian Economic History Review, 60*(3), 309–334.

Di Matteo, L., Green, D., Owens, A., Shanahan, M., & McAloon, J. (2012, November 1–4). *Resources, Land Abundance and Inequality. Understanding Wealth-Holding and Investment in Britain and Its Settler Colonies, 1870–1930.* SSHA meetings Vancouver.

Di Matteo, L. (2013a). Women, Wealth and Economic Change: An Assessment of the Impact of Women's Property Law in Wentworth County, Ontario, 1872–1927. *Explorations in Economic History, 50*, 285–307.

Di Matteo, L. (2016a). Wealth Distribution and the Canadian Middle Class: Historical Evidence and Policy Implications. *Canadian Public Policy, 42*(2), 132–151.

Di Matteo, L. (2016b). All Equal in the Sight of God: Economic Inequality and Religion in the Early Twentieth Century. *European Review of Economic History, 20*, 23–45.

Gallman, R. E. (1969). Trends in the Size Distribution of Wealth in the Nineteenth Century: Some Speculations. In L. Soltow (Ed.), *Six Papers on the Size Distribution of Wealth and Income.* New York: National Bureau of Economic Research.

Garbinti, B., Goupille-Lebret, J., & Piketty, T. (2016). *Accounting for Wealth Inequality Dynamics: Methods, Estimates and Simulations for France (1800–2014).* World Wealth and Income Database, Working Paper No. 2016/5.

Goodman, W. D. (1995). Death Taxes in Canada, in the Past and in the Possible Future. *Canadian Tax Journal, 43*(5), 1360–1376.

Gwyn, J., & Siddiq, F. K. (1992). Wealth Distribution in Nova Scotia During the Confederation Era, 1851 and 1871. *Canadian Historical Review, LXXIII*(4), 435–452.

Hardle, W. (1991). *Applied Nonparametric Regression, Econometric Society Monographs* (Vol. 19). Cambridge: Cambridge University Press.

Johnson, B. W., & Eller, M. B. (1998). Federal Taxation of Inheritance and Wealth Transfers. In R. K. Miller & S. J. McNamee (Eds.), *Inheritance and Wealth in America* (pp. 61–90). New York: Plenum Press.

Jones, A. H. (1980). *Wealth of A Nation to Be: The American Colonies on the Eve of the Revolution.* New York: Columbia Press.

Kennickell, A. (2009). *Ponds and Streams: Wealth and Income in the U.S., 1989 to 2007*. Finance and Economics Discussion Series 2009-13, Board of Governors of the Federal Reserve System (U.S.).

Kennickell, A. (2011). *Tossed and Turned: Wealth Dynamics of U.S. Households 2007–2009*. Finance and Economics Discussion Series 2011-51, Board of Governors of the Federal Reserve System (U.S.).

Kopczuk, W., & Saez, E. (2004). Top Wealth Shares in the United States, 1916–2000: Evidence from Estate Tax Returns. *National Tax Journal, 57*(2), 445–487.

Lindert, P. H. (1986). Unequal English Wealth Since 1670. *The Journal of Political Economy, 94*(6), 1127–1162.

Lindert, P. H. (2000). Three Centuries of Inequality in Britain and America. In A. B. Atkinson & F. Bourguignon (Eds.), *Handbook of Income Distribution* (Vol. 1). Amsterdam: North-Holland.

Oja, G. (1987). *Changes in the Distribution of Wealth in Canada, 1970–1984*. Statistics Canada, 13-588, No. 1.

Osberg, L. (1984). *Economic Inequality in the United States*. Armonk: M.E. Sharpe Ltd.

Perry, J. H. (1984). *Taxation in Canada, Fourth Edition*. Canadian Tax Paper No. 74, Canadian Tax Foundation, Toronto.

Perry, J. H. (1989). *A Fiscal History of Canada-The Postwar Years*. Canadian Tax Paper No. 85, Canadian Tax Foundation, Toronto.

Pfeffer, F. T., Danziger, S., & Schoeni, R. F. (2013). Wealth Disparities Before and After the Great Recession. *The Annals of the American Academy of Political and Social Science, 650*(1), 98–123.

Piketty, T. (2014). *Capital in the 21st Century*. Cambridge, MA: Harvard University Press.

Reed, H. (2014, May 29). Piketty, Chris Giles and Wealth on Equality: It's All About the Discontinuities. *The Guardian*. https://www.theguardian.com/news/datablog/2014/may/29/piketty-chris-giles-and-wealthinequality-its-all-about-the-discontinuities

Roine, J., & Waldenström, D. (2014, April). *Long-Run Trends in the Distribution of Income and Wealth* (IZA DP No. 1857).

Roine, J., & Waldenström, D. (2015). Long-Run Trends in the Distribution of Income and Wealth. In A. B. Atkinson & F. Bourguignon (Eds.), *Handbook of Income Distribution* (Vol. 2A). North-Holland, Amsterdam: Elsevier.

Rowlingson, K. (2012, December), *Wealth Inequality: Key Facts*. Policy Commission on the Distribution of Wealth, University of Birmingham. http://www.birmingham.ac.uk/Documents/research/SocialSciences/Key-Facts-Background-Paper-BPCIV.pdf

Saez, E., & Zucman, G. (2016). Wealth Inequality in the United States Since 1913: Evidence from Capitalized Income Tax Data. *The Quarterly Journal of Economics, 131*(2), 519–578.

Shammas, C. (1993). A New Look at Long-Term Trends in Wealth Inequality in the United States. *The American Historical Review, 98*(2), 412–431.

Siddiq, F. K. (1988). The Size Distribution of Probate Wealth-Holdings in Nova Scotia in the Late 19th Century. *Acadiensis, 18*(1), 136–147.

Soltow, L. (1989). *Distribution of Wealth and Income in the United States in 1798*. Pittsburgh: University of Pittsburgh Press.

Vermuelen, P. (2016). Estimating the Top Tail of the Wealth Distribution. *American Economic Review: Papers and Proceedings, 106*(5), 646–650.

Wolff, E. N. (1987). Estimates of Household Wealth Inequality in the U.S. 1962–1983. *Review of Income and Wealth, 33*(3), 231–256.

Wolff, E. N. (1991). The Distribution of Household Wealth: Methodological Issues, Time Trends, and Cross-Sectional Comparisons. In L. Osberg (Ed.), *Economic Inequality and Poverty: International Perspectives* (pp. 92–133). New York: M.E. Sharpe, Inc.

Wolff, E. N. (1994). Trends in Household Wealth in the United States, 1962–83 and 1983–89. *Review of Income and Wealth, 40*(2), 143–174.

Wolff, E. N. (1996). International Comparisons of Wealth Inequality. *Review of Income and Wealth, 42*(4), 433–451.

CHAPTER 4

# Understanding the Determinants of Wealth Inequality

**Abstract** Determinants of inequality depend on the ability to take advantage of economic opportunities and responses to economic shocks. The Kuznets inverted u-shaped curve maintains that inequality worsens during industrialization and improves afterward. Other factors are public policy regarding taxes, including wealth taxation and government spending, labor force skills and unionization, institutions, education, resource endowments, and demographic factors such as aging and cohort size. Globalization, portfolio composition, home ownership rates, technological revolutions, changes in factor returns, wars, and economic shocks—as well as changes in economic growth patterns—are also factors. These factors can either push inequality up or pull it down with the long-term trend the outcome of a resultant between these forces, some of which exhibiting both push and pull tendencies at points in or over time.

**Keywords** Kuznets • Determinants • Estate taxation • Push • Pull

The complex long-term determinants of inequality ultimately depend on individuals and families being able to take advantage of economic opportunities as well as their ability to absorb economic shocks. Any study of inequality using historical micro-data must inevitably be examined via some focus on Simon Kuznet's (1955, 1966) work on the inverted U hypothesis



L. Di Matteo, *The Evolution and Determinants of Wealth Inequality in the North Atlantic Anglo-Sphere, 1668–2013*, https://doi.org/10.1007/978-3-319-89773-8_4

regarding the relationship between economic growth and inequality, which was based on income distribution data for the United States and the United Kingdom. In the Kuznets explanation, economic inequality worsens during the initial industrialization and development growth burst in an economy and then declines as industrialization is completed, the economy matures and the growth rate slows.

Milanovic (2016) builds on this approach in terms of looking at inequality as moving in broad cycles and sees inequality as a result of a series of long-term waves of Kuznets growth cycles. Studies finding a Kuznets type relationship in an American context also include Williamson (1965), Lindert and Williamson (1985), Williamson and Lindert (1980), and Lindert (1991). For Canada, Alan Green (1967, 1968/1969, 1971) found evidence of a Kuznets curve with regional income disparities converging after World War I. At the same time, the Kuznets Curve is by no means uncontroversial, and there is also a body of literature that finds weak empirical support for the relationship.[1]

Williamson (1996a, b, 1998) and Higgins and Williamson (2002) move beyond examining inequality as a simple unconditional Kuznets curve relationship and consider that along with changes in income or wealth, inequality is also affected by public policy, labor force skills, institutions,[2] education, resource endowments, and demographic factors—including age structure.[3] For example, Higgins and Williamson (2002) find the relative size of the population cohort aged between 40 and 59 years has a negative and significant effect on inequality. This relationship may indeed reflect life-cycle effects with respect to age as wealth does rise over the course of the life cycle.[4] Atack and Bateman (1981) and Gallman (1978) argue that because wealth rises with age, the larger the proportion of young people in a society, the more wealth inequality there would be.[5]

Roine and Waldenström (2015) in their search for inequality explanations offer the effects of broad global developments such as globalization, technological revolutions and changes in factor returns, wars, and economic shocks, as well as changes in patterns of economic growth. The role of economic growth may also be a factor in wealth inequality as there is some evidence that declining wealth inequality is sometimes a feature of periods of slower economic growth, while periods of rapid economic growth are accompanied by rising inequality—in other words, economic booms may generate inequality while economic downturns may reduce it.[6]

Deaton (2013) also notes that periods of rapid economic growth and change can be associated with greater economic inequality in that economic innovation and grow must start somewhere and therefore differences in the timing of economic growth can result in divergences in wealth and hence its distribution. There is also the relationship between the share of income derived from capital and capital gains[7] and the effects of public policy via the taxation of income[8] and wealth. Time periods that generate large increases in capital income and capital gains can be associated with rising inequality, and the policy response to those increases can affect wealth inequality.

At the same time, there are dissenting views that argue that periods of rapid or fast economic growth do not necessarily trigger greater inequality. Alfani and Ryckbosch (2016) and Alfani and Ammannati (2017) note that inequality in European regions was already growing prior to the rapid economic growth of industrialization and may have been the result of poor democratic institutions and social spending differences.[9] Ryckbosch (2017) examines data from 15 towns in the Low Countries—between 1400 and 1900—and finds growing urban inequality prior to the rapid per capita income growth of the industrial revolution and attributes it to changes in the functional distribution of income away from labor and toward capital rather than the economic growth process per se.

The relationship between economic growth and inequality is of course highlighted in the work of Thomas Piketty (2014), whose general theory of wealth accumulation and inequality highlights the crucial relationship between the rate of economic growth and the return on wealth or capital. In general, using the expression $r > g$ (where r is the rate of return to wealth and g is the economic growth rate), the return to wealth (r) growing faster than economic output (g) results in rising inequality. Rentier societies in particular thrive when $r > g$, as, for example, in the case of Paris from 1870 to 1930.[10] Given that the long-term return to capital has historically averaged close to 4 percent while the rate of growth of per capita GDP is about 2 percent, this suggests a natural tendency toward greater wealth inequality in support of Piketty's view.

For example, data from the Jordà-Schularick-Taylor Macrohistory Database, a comprehensive macro-financial panel dataset of 17 countries spanning the periods 1870–2013[11] shows that average real per capita GDP across these countries—even for the entire period 1870 to 2013—has averaged 2 percent. However, a notable exception is evident once the growth rates are broken up by time period. Average annual real per capita

GDP growth across these 17 countries was 1.6 percent from 1871 to 1913, 1.7 percent from 1914 to 1945, 4.1 percent from 1946 to 1973, and 1.8 percent from 1974 to 2013.[12]

By comparison, average short-term interest rates from the Jordà-Schularick-Taylor Macrohistory Database were 4.2 percent from 1871 to 1913, 4.3 percent from 1914 to 1945, 4.2 percent from 1946 to 1973, and 6.5 percent from 1974 to 2013. The gap between r and g is the least in the period from 1945 to 1973. Thus, one might expect reduced wealth inequality during the higher economic growth post-war era of the twentieth century up until the oil-shock induced slowdown of the 1970s, and indeed this portion of the twentieth century has been marked by relatively lower wealth inequality.

Therefore, according to Piketty's work, all other things being equal, faster economic growth may reduce the importance of wealth in a society and result in greater equality, but slower growth will serve to increase it. Given historical rates of economic growth and asset returns, the natural tendency therefore would be for increased wealth inequality over time, barring the impact of any positive economic growth shocks as a result of economic factors such as technological or demographic change, government policies to reduce wealth concentration via tax or social policy, or economic shocks that lower the return to capital such as war.

The effects of economic shocks such as war[13] are certainly noted in the work of Piketty et al. (2006), Piketty (2000), Piketty and Saez (2013), Piketty and Zucman (2013), and Piketty (2014) in terms of their effects on top income and wealth holders. Indeed, Piketty (2014) makes a strong case that increasing equality during the course of the first half of the twentieth century was at best an aberration brought about by the destruction of war, which eroded the return to capital. Indeed, it has been argued that catastrophe is the major historical factor that has curbed inequality, whether they be plagues, revolutions, wars, or collapsed states that have upended existing social orders and affected wealth distributions.[14] Periods of war have also resulted in debt accumulation and rapid money creation that fueled inflation, which can also affect wealth and the return to capital.[15]

In the case of the North Atlantic Anglosphere, the United Kingdom bore the more direct military brunt of destruction from bombings and attacks during both World Wars, while the United States and Canada despite the economic effects on their production and resource allocation escaped the more severe infrastructure and capital damaging effects of direct attack. In Britain, for example, the value of national capital between 1914 and 1945 fell from a range of about six and a half to seven years of the value of national income to about two and a half years.[16]

While greater inequality is associated with wartime destruction of capital, that would not have been the case in Canada or the United States or for that matter countries like Switzerland or Sweden—which also see declines in inequality in the twentieth century. At the same time, there would have been government intervention in the economy to fund the war effort—such as more aggressive taxation—which would have disrupted private sector wealth accumulation. For example, World War I in Canada saw the introduction of the personal and corporate income taxes and World War II in Canada saw particularly aggressive increases in the income tax rates, making the system very progressive and a factor in the post-war decline in inequality.[17]

In the case of the United States, even the Civil War is also seen as having some leveling effect on wealth inequality. Dupont and Rosenbloom (2016) argue that although there was an entrenched southern planter elite that retained their economic status even after the war, the turmoil of 1860s nevertheless opened greater opportunities for mobility in the South than was the case in the North, resulting in much greater turnover among wealthy southerners than among comparably wealthy northerners. The Civil War decade created greater opportunities for those with moderate wealth in 1860—between the 55th and 90th percentiles—to move up to the top of the wealth distribution. Nearly 40 percent of the wealthiest southerners in 1870 had been in this group in 1860, compared to less than one quarter of the richest northerners.

Related to war, taxes, and government intervention in the economy are of course the changes in the size and role of the state in all three countries during the course of the twentieth century, which saw an expansion of government.[18] While the war eras are associated with spikes in public sector size in all three countries, there has also been a long-term general expansion of government relative to GDP, which peaked in the 1970s. The average central government expenditure to GDP ratio between 1870 and 1913 was 2.4 percent in the United States, 7.3 percent in the United Kingdom, and 6.5 percent in Canada. The era of the Great Depression and World War II generated pressure for a greater role for government, and during the period 1946–1973, the average central government expenditure to GDP ratio averaged 17 percent in the United States, 27.6 percent in the United Kingdom, and 16.4 percent in Canada.[19] All three countries saw some moderation in the size of their overall public sectors after the 1980s and especially during the 1990s.[20] This expansion was also accompanied by a shift in the composition of spending in all three countries toward health, education, and social welfare.[21]

It should be noted that in the case of Canada and the United States,[22] these government size figures are also underestimates given their federal nature, and their ratios of general government expenditure to GDP are even higher. For example, in Canada, until World War I, the federal share of total government spending was approximately 40 percent. After the peak of over 70 percent reached during World War I, the federal share came down quickly but went up again during the Depression era and soared during World War II, reaching over 90 percent. The Canadian federal share of spending came down more gradually after World War II—leveling off at almost 50 percent during the 1970s and 1980s before falling once again to about 40 percent during the 1990s.[23]

Another potential variable affecting wealth distribution is the manner in which wealth is held—or portfolio composition. Portfolio composition can affect asset returns and the subsequent distribution of wealth. Financial assets are less equally distributed than non-financial assets, especially if owner-occupied housing is a major component of wealth. Also, there is a tendency for the portfolio share of equities to increase with wealth level and for housing wealth to be a more important component of middle classes of wealth and income as opposed to higher wealth deciles.[24] For example, Skott (2011) finds that the low- and middle-income classes tend to hold fewer financial assets, which has been a factor in increasing inequality.

Changes in asset prices and rates of return to assets can have a major impact on the distribution of wealth based on differences in asset holding across wealth levels.[25] Indeed, the fall in home values in the United States between 2007 and 2012 reduced household net worth disproportionately for middle-class wealth holders as they had larger shares of their assets in housing as opposed to the wealthiest members of society who had more of their wealth in financial assets.[26]

Related to portfolio composition is the impact of home ownership on wealth inequality. Owning a home can be a substantial asset, and home ownership rates in Canada, the United States, and the United Kingdom have varied over time, though home ownership rates are now higher in all three countries relative to the past. For example, in the United States in 1890, the proportion of owner-occupied homes was 47.8 percent, reached

50 percent during World War II, and continued growing to reach 62.9 percent by 1970.[27] It continued to rise peaking at 69 percent in 2006 just before the US subprime market crisis and has since declined to reach just over 63 percent in 2017.[28] Canadian home ownership rates have historically been slightly below American rates but with growth paralleling those of the United States quite closely and reaching 50 percent after World War II. By 1971, home ownership rates in Canada were at 60.3 percent, and they have continued to rise despite the 2008–2009 global financial crisis and subprime market crisis in the United States, reaching 69 percent by 2011.[29]

Homeownership rates in the United Kingdom were historically much lower than the United States and Canada, as there was a greater tendency to rent rather than own accommodation. In 1918, the vast majority of households in England and Wales rented, with only about 23 percent of homes being owner occupied. Home ownership rates grew slowly but then began growing more rapidly after 1950. By 1971, there was an equal percentage of households owning and renting, and ownership continued to increase, reaching a peak of 69 percent in 2001. However, by 2013, the ownership rate had fallen to 64 percent.[30] The increase in home ownership rates in the United Kingdom appears to have occurred particularly after the onset of some significant changes that affected the British housing market, known as 'Right to Buy' policies. Under the Housing Act of 1980, there were incentives provided to public housing or council house tenants, which enabled them to buy their homes at a discount.[31]

The question is what the effects of increased home ownership over time have been on wealth inequality. Home ownership is more of a middle-class asset, whereas higher wealth deciles emphasize financial assets more. Given the mitigation of wealth inequality in the first half of the twentieth century, one can indeed make the case that reduced wealth inequality is also correlated with more dispersed and indeed higher rates of home ownership. At the same time, Rognlie (2015) has suggested that much of the increase in US wealth inequality over the last few decades was actually driven by the increase in the share of capital held in housing stock. Indeed, the rising real cost of residential investment and the limited supplies of residential land have conspired to make housing more expensive and made it a rising share of wealth and income. As a result, the impact of home ownership rates on wealth inequality is possibly non-linear, first with falling inequality as ownership rates rise and then growing inequality as the ownership rates exceed higher rates such as 50 percent.

Of course, the historically higher rates of real property ownership in Canada and the United States relative to the United Kingdom may also be a reflection of natural resource abundance and particularly land abundance as a result of frontier settlement. Another related ingredient of portfolio composition's contribution to historic wealth inequality is the effect of individual windfalls in wealth as a result of natural resource revenues or land endowments acquired during settlement phases. The United States, Canada, and the rest of the Americas, as well as Australia and New Zealand, are European settler economies, and settlers often were the recipients of grants of either *free*[32] or heavily subsidized land. Both Canada and the United States had land grant programs in the nineteenth and early twentieth centuries that provided real estate wealth, and in the Canadian case, some evidence suggests that higher and more dispersed rates of land ownership in the West may have mitigated nineteenth-century inequality.[33] At the same time, other North American studies of nineteenth-century wealth accumulation document high rates of accumulation as well as high wealth inequality, even in frontier areas of recent settlement where such land grant programs would have been in effect.[34]

Yet, there is also some evidence supporting greater wealth equality in more farming and agriculturally intensive economies. For example, over the period 1870–1930, wealth inequality in Canada was less pronounced in agricultural frontier Manitoba relative to industrialized Ontario, with higher rates of land ownership and greater farm employment as key factors in the difference.[35] Indeed, nineteenth-century North American farm economies may have afforded a reasonable standard of living to people of relatively modest means even if it meant they were in the lower end of the wealth distribution.

In the case of the United States, this would embody the 'Jeffersonian' vision of a relatively egalitarian rural society of stout yeoman.[36] For example, southeastern Pennsylvania in the eighteenth century was a rural society with growing inequality, and yet a large proportion of the population could be characterized as neither rich nor poor. Lemon (1972) documents how the average farmer in Pennsylvania was able to produce sufficient output to provide for their family and, at the same time, generate a surplus of produce that could be marketed, thereby generating a reasonably high level of material welfare.

Another factor affecting wealth distribution and economic inequality in general is changes in the labor market and the return to labor that affects income and ultimately wealth accumulation. Piketty (2014: 240–241) notes that for nineteenth-century France, work and study alone 'were not enough to achieve the same level of comfort afforded by inherited wealth and the income derived from it', but the period after World War II saw income from work and acquired human capital become of greater importance. Indeed, the twentieth century saw income from labor grow and become more secure facilitating wealth accumulation, thereby making these changes a factor in the more egalitarian distribution of wealth during the twentieth century. Stiglitz (2012) recently has noted that in the globalized economy, wage earners are given relatively unfavorable treatment compared to financial capital, as the policies that have increased inequality have not been shaped by wage earners or their unions, which have declined in importance.

As a result, one might expect that another key factor is twentieth-century labor markets and unionization, which is correlated with higher and more stable incomes and then potential spillovers on broader-based wealth accumulation, with effects on both income and wealth distribution. In response to the poor working conditions of the late nineteenth century in terms of long hours and safety conditions, unions began to form in Canada, the United States, and the United Kingdom. Unions generally fought for higher wages, more reasonable hours of work, as well as safer working conditions, particularly in the developing manufacturing and industrial sector. In the case of wage inequality and income distribution, evidence comparing Canada, the United States, and the United Kingdom has found that unions tend to decrease wage inequality among men and have an equalizing effect on the dispersion of wages across skill groups in all three countries.[37]

In recent decades, American, Canadian, and UK union membership as a percentage of wage and salary earners has been declining, like much of the rest of the OECD.[38] In 1980, union members as a share of wage and salary workers was 51.7 percent in the United Kingdom, 34 percent in Canada, and 22.1 percent in the United States, with an OECD average of 34.1 percent. By 2014, the percentages were 25.1 percent for the United Kingdom, 26.4 percent for Canada, and 10.7 percent for the United States, with an OECD average of 16.7 percent. This suggests another potential determinant of changing inequality in the twentieth century.

In the United Kingdom, trade union activity started with the Owenite and Chartist movements of the 1830s and 1840s, but more permanent unions were created in industrial and textile sectors starting in the 1850s. The Royal Commission on Trade Unions in 1867 formally recognized trade union activity, and it was legalized in 1871 with the adoption of the Trade Union Act. Membership grew afterward, but peak memberships and expansion periods occurred after World War II. Figure 4.1 plots both total union membership and the percentage of employment in a trade union, and the two lines move quite closely together.[39]

In the United Kingdom, total union membership in 1892 was 1.576 million, and as a share of employment, trade union membership was 10.5 percent. This rose quite steeply to peak immediately after World War I at 8.348 million members and 41.3 percent in 1920, before declining to a

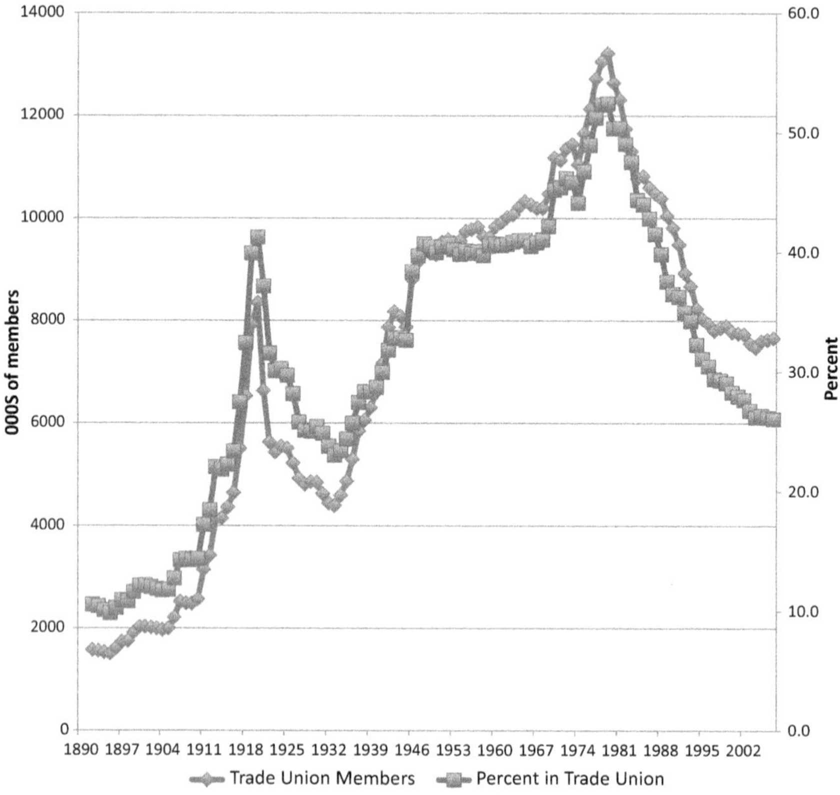


**Fig. 4.1** Trade union membership and density in the United Kingdom, 1892–2007. (Source: Guardian Trade Union Database. https://www.theguardian.com/news/datablog/2010/apr/30/union-membership-data#data)

low of 4.392 million and 23 percent by 1933. Growth then resumed and peaked in 1979 at 13.212 members and a share of employment at 52.4 percent. A decline then sets in, and by 2007, total membership was down to 7.656 million and a 26.1 percent employment share.

The North American trade union experience paralleled that of the United Kingdom. In the United States, the American Federation of Labor (AFL) began in the 1880s and was followed by the Congress of Industrial Organizations (CIO) in the 1930s, and then a merger between the two in the 1950s created the AFL-CIO. The Canadian labor union movement began in the 1870s, and the Trades and Labor Congress was established in the 1880s, which later evolved into the Canadian Congress of Labor in 1940.[40]

Between 1920 and 1960, union growth in Canada was also similar to the United States. There was an expansion in membership during World War II, and union membership in the United States peaked during the 1960s, before beginning a decline that persisted into the twenty-first century. A similar expansion occurs in Canada, but after the mid-1960s, Canadian union membership expanded and only began to decline in the 1990s. As a share of wage and salary workers, American union membership peaked in the late 1950s at just under 35 percent (and at just below 28 percent as a share of total employed workers), while Canadian membership peaks in the late 1980s at just under 40 percent.[41]

Figure 4.2 plots American trade union members and the percentage of total workers who were unionized from 1930 to 2003.[42] Unlike the United Kingdom, the two series do not move in tandem, with total membership peaking in 1979 at 20.986 million, while membership as a percentage of total employed workers peaked much earlier—in 1954—at 28.3 percent. By 2003, total union membership in the United States was down to 15.766 million, while as a percentage of total employed workers, it had fallen to 11.5 percent—a share not seen since the late 1930s.

Figure 4.3 plots Canadian union membership rates from 1920 to 2014 based on two sources: Riddell (1993) and the OECD.[43] The two series overlap for the 1980–1990 period and are similar, with the OECD shares slightly lower than the Riddell numbers. The Riddell numbers show Canadian union membership peaking in 1985 at 38.1 percent followed by a decline, whereas the OECD numbers show a peak in 1982 at 36.8 percent and then a decline. A feature of the Canadian experience is the rising share of public sector workers among union membership in the late twentieth and into twenty-first centuries.[44]

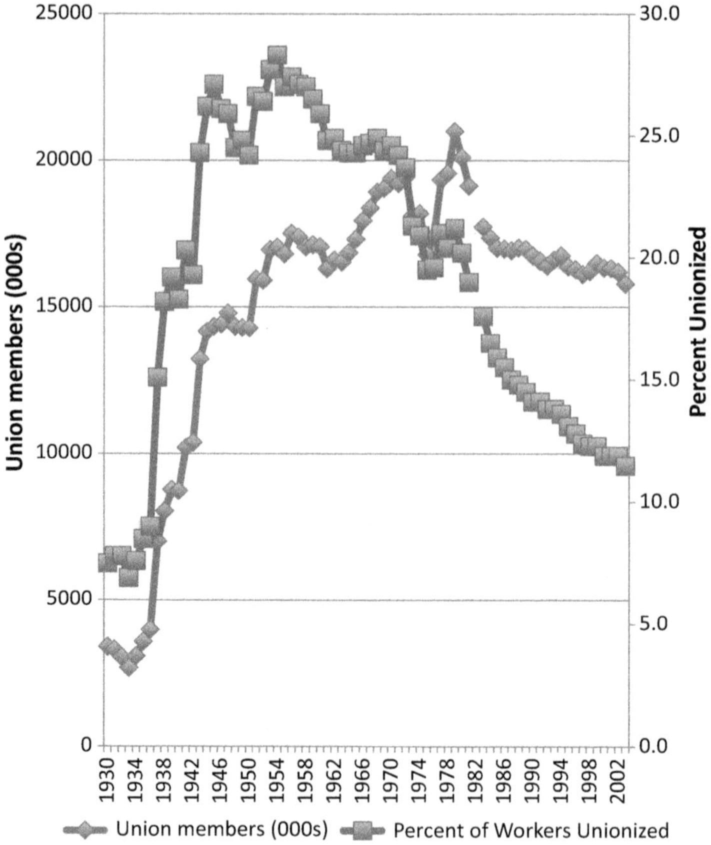


**Fig. 4.2** Trade union membership and density in the United States, 1930–2003. (Source: Mayer (2004: 22–23))

Another key institutional factor—often manifesting itself via public policy changes—that affects the long-term evolution of economic inequality and especially wealth inequality[45] is the system of inheritance and, of course, estate taxation.[46] In the North Atlantic Anglosphere, the system of inheritance is rooted in British property transmission institutions, with a key feature being primogeniture—the eldest son receiving the bulk of the inheritance—that functioned to enhance long-term dynastic wealth accumulation and played a role in fostering inequality.[47] In the land-rich settler

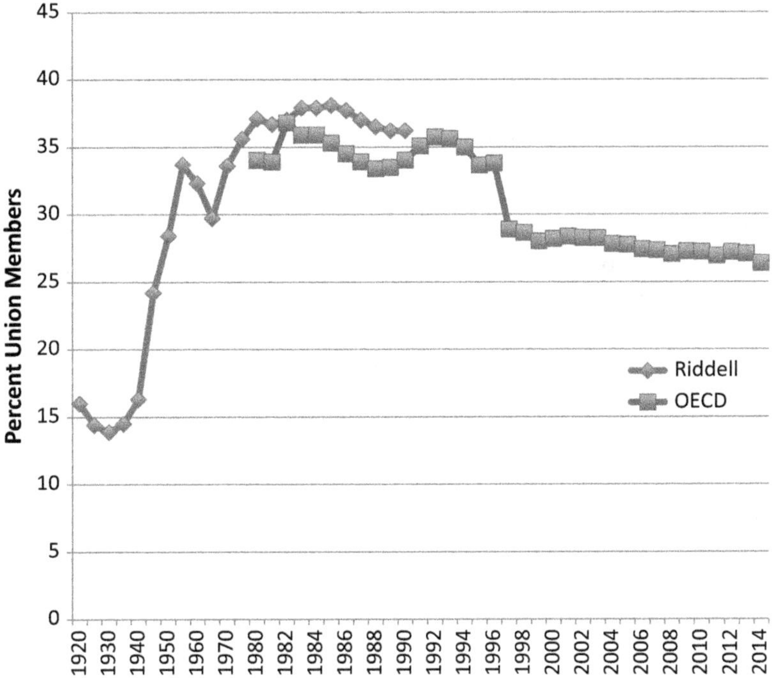


**Fig. 4.3** Trade union density in Canada, 1920–2014. (Data Sources: Riddell (1993) and OECD STAT)

countries such as Canada and the United States, the purpose of inheritance shifted toward providing offspring with a start in life in return for old-age support and moved inheritance systems more toward multigeniture.[48] In all of these three countries, the evidence and social perception of rising wealth inequality ultimately brought about the calls for estate taxation.

While Canada, the United States, and the United Kingdom all bring in wealth taxes on the property of the deceased by the middle of the twentieth century, these taxes are all either eliminated, reduced substantially, or exempted amounts raised starting in the 1970s. Indeed, there has been a tendency for wealth and inheritance taxes to fall out of favor around the world, with the golden age of inheritance taxation as measured by the revenue share of government peaking in the early twentieth century.[49] For

Canada, the federal estate taxes are in effect from 1941 to 1973.[50] For the United States, the modern system and higher rates are in effect from 1916 to 1977, with reductions in wealth taxation rates taking effect after 1977. In the United Kingdom, the modern estate tax system with a jump in rates starts in 1894, and a period of declines in the rate begin in 1981. Thus, for all three countries, we have a period of relatively higher or effective estate taxation that can be used as a determinant variable for wealth inequality.

The discussion of the determinants of wealth inequality can be quite detailed but can be usefully summarized into a brief analytical framework of *push-pull* factors affecting inequality. Push-pull models are a part of the literature regarding the determinants of migration, which attempts to explain migration across location as per their attractiveness in terms of pulling migrants in or pushing them out.[51] We can argue that the forces driving changes in wealth distribution can be similarly categorized into economic, social, demographic, and institutional push-pull factors. All of these factors can be seen to either push inequality up or pull it down thereby making the long-term trend the outcome of a resultant between these forces some of which can exhibit both push and pull tendencies at points in time or over time. Added to these factors are explicit public policies, especially via the tax system, designed to affect the distribution of income and wealth, which can serve to either pull down inequality or indeed even push it up.

Figure 4.4 provides a brief diagrammatic summary of a push-pull framework explaining the drivers of wealth inequality over the long term. For example, the process of economic growth, industrialization, and development generates economic growth, and rapid economic growth has been documented as correlated with rising wealth inequality. Thus, rapid economic growth can be seen as a factor pushing up wealth inequality. At the same time, slower economic growth can be correlated with moderating wealth inequality and would therefore be a factor pulling it down. Other economic shocks such as war or natural disasters can also have effects on wealth inequality, which based on the literature surveyed can pull it down.

Social and demographic factors broadly defined such as the age distribution of the population, gender distribution, family size, as well as educational and human attributes of population are additional factors. These can be accompanied by institutional factors such as systems of land holding, banking and financial systems, unionization, religion, government, and estate transmission, as well as public policies designed to affect these

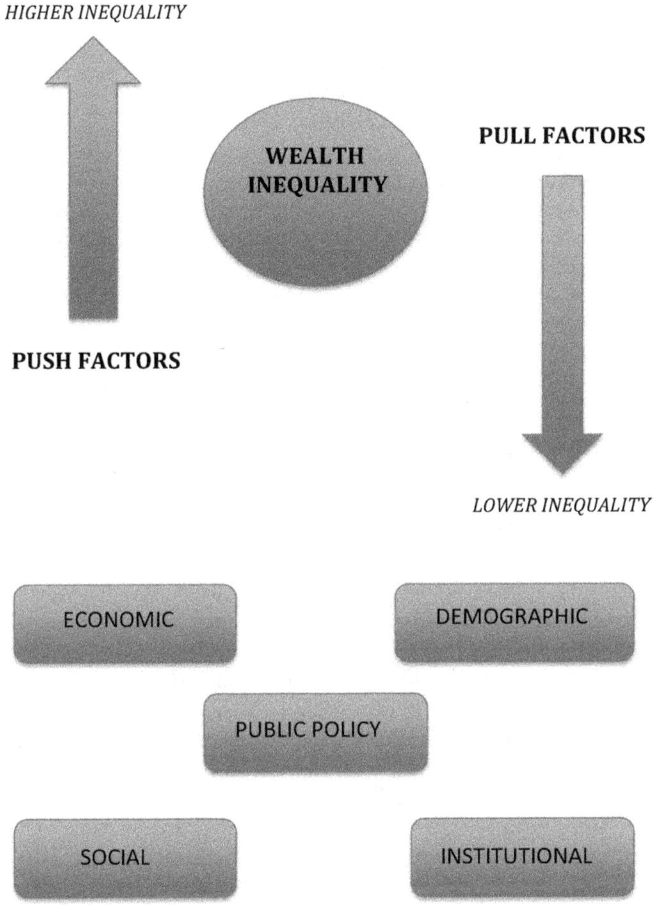


**Fig. 4.4** A push-pull framework for understanding the evolution of wealth inequality

variables. Again, these demographic and institutional factors can have either positive or negative effects on wealth inequality, with the ultimate impact a resultant of competing forces. And of course, all of these factors—economic, social, demographic, and institutional—can be influenced by public policies whether they are government tax policies or other types of regulations and incentives.

## Notes

1. For an overview of some of this literature, see Gallup (2012) as well as Deininger and Squire (1998), Savvidesa and Stengos (2000), Atkinson and Brandolini (2001), and Barro (2000, 2008).
2. Along with government, other types of social institutions can also affect wealth and inequality. For example, religious affiliation can also be a factor in wealth accumulation as well as its distribution, if they influence activities such as savings, child bearing, and inheritance. See Di Matteo (2016b).
3. As another example, Spain sees a fall in income inequality during the opening phases of its economy opening up to international competition from the 1850s to the 1890s and then a rise in inequality from the 1890s to the start of World War I, which coincided with a return to protectionism. See Escosura (2008).
4. Life-cycle saving is the accumulation of assets during productive years to finance consumption during a period of non-income earning activity. See Ando and Modigliani (1963), Bernheim et al. (1985), and Modigliani (1988a, b).
5. For additional detail examining the link between age structure and wealth inequality, see Di Matteo (2001).
6. Certainly, evidence for Canada also suggests periods of rapid economic growth like the wheat boom era were also associated with rising inequality. See Di Matteo (2012).
7. Armour et al. (2013) and Burkhauser et al. (2013) use survey evidence from household panels in the United States and Australia to study the effect of realized and unrealized capital gains on income inequality and conclude that they are important drivers of inequality.
8. For example, Saez and Veall (2005) showed that Canadian top income shares were negatively correlated with top marginal income tax rates.
9. The Economic Inequality Across Italy and Europe Research Project (EINITE) headed by Guido Alfani, and including researchers Francesco Ammannati, Matteo Di Tullion, Roberta Frigeri, Hector Garcia Monero, Sergio Sardone and Davide De Franco, Fabrice Boudjaaba, Carlos Santiago-Caballero, and Wouter Ryckbosch housed at Bocconi University, has as its main research questions the relationship between economic inequality and economic growth.
10. Pikkety et al. (2014).
11. These countries include Australia, Belgium, Canada, Denmark, Finland, France, Germany, Italy, Japan, Netherlands, Norway, Portugal, Spain, Sweden, Switzerland, United Kingdom, and the United States. The data set and documentation are available at: http://www.macrohistory.net/data. Accessed October 2016. Òscar Jordà, Moritz Schularick, and Alan

M. Taylor. 2017. 'Macrofinancial History and the New Business Cycle Facts'. *NBER Macroeconomics Annual 2016*, volume 31, edited by Martin Eichenbaum and Jonathan A. Parker. Chicago: University of Chicago Press.

12. Calculations by author.
13. Along with the shock of war, plague and pestilence may also be factors. Alfani and Ammannati (2017) note declining inequality in the Florentine state in the wake of the Black Death from 1348 to 1349.
14. Scheidel (2017a, b).
15. Piketty (2014: 106–109).
16. Piketty (2014: 147).
17. During World War II, Canadian income tax rates soared. The pre-World War II marginal tax rate on taxable income between $1000 and $2000 in the dollars of the day was 4 percent. By 1942, it had increased to 44 percent. For taxable income between $10,000 and $15,000, it was 13.7 percent before the war, but fully 69 percent by 1942. See Di Matteo (2017b).
18. The growth of the public sector is also an area of substantial scholarship. Two key explanations are Wagner's Law and the Peacock-Wiseman Displacement Hypothesis. Wagner's Law maintains government expenditure grows faster than income in industrializing countries because government expenditures such as social welfare expenditures are income elastic. Peacock and Wiseman argue that the growth of public spending is driven by taxpayer tolerance of taxation and this tolerance is greater during times of national or social crisis such as war. See Wagner (1893, 1894) and Peacock and Wiseman (1967). See also Tanzi (2011) for an overview of the changing role of the state.
19. Author's calculations from data obtained from the Jorda-Schularick-Taylor Macro History Database. See: The data set and documentation are available at: http://www.macrohistory.net/data. Oscar Jorda, Moritz Schularick, and Alan M. Taylor. 2017. 'Macrofinancial History and the New Business Cycle Facts'. NBER Macroeconomics Annual 2016, volume 31, edited by Martin Eichenbaum and Jonathan A. Parker. Chicago: University of Chicago Press.
20. See Di Matteo (2013b: 4). For a discussion of Canadian inequality trends and public sector activity see Di Matteo (2016a)
21. In the subsequent regression work of the next section, government size is not explicitly controlled for given the heavy correlation of this expansion with the post-war economic boom variable and the contraction of the government sector with the second era of globalization, as well as the relaxation of estate tax regimes after 1970.
22. For the United States, data from the *Historical Statistics of the United States, Colonial Times to 1970* for the period 1890–1970, and OECD numbers for the post-1990 period, suggest increase in the federal share of total

government spending over time. For the period 1870–1938, the average federal share was approximately 40 percent. By the late 1990s, the federal share of total government spending in the United States exceeded 50 percent. By comparison, in the late 1990s, numbers from the OECD show that the central government share of expenditure in the United Kingdom—traditionally more centralized—was 90 percent, whereas by 2013, it has declined to just over 80 percent.

23. See http://www.macleans.ca/economy/economicanalysis/the-most-important-economic-charts-to-watch-in-2018/#liviodimatteo
24. Davies/Shorrocks, 'Distribution' (2000: 643–644).
25. For example, the Royal Commission on the Distribution of Income and Wealth (1979) for the United Kingdom found the reduction in the wealth share of the top tiers of the wealth distribution over the 1972–1976 period to be the result of a rise in land prices and a drop in the stock market.
26. Landy (2013).
27. Historical Statistics of the United States, Colonial Times to 1970, Series N238-245. See: https://www.census.gov/library/publications/1975/compendia/hist_stats_colonial-1970.html
28. Source: Federal Reserve Economic Data. RHORUSQ156N: Homeownership Rate for the United States, Percent, Quarterly, Not Seasonally Adjusted.
29. See: Statistics Canada (2013) National Household Survey: Income and Housing—Homeownership and Shelter Costs in Canada, National Household Survey year 2011 (99-014-X). http://www12.statcan.gc.ca/nhs-enm/2011/as-sa/99-014-x/2011002/c-g/c-g01-eng.cfm
30. See: http://webarchive.nationalarchives.gov.uk/20160107120359/http://www.ons.gov.uk/ons/rel/census/2011-census-analysis/a-century-of-home-ownership-and-renting-in-england-and-wales/short-story-on-housing.html
31. Disney and Luo (2014).
32. Of course, nothing is ever actually free. Recipients of land grants nonetheless had to commit to working the land for a given period of time and often even paid a small nominal fee.
33. Di Matteo (2012).
34. See, for example, Gregson (1996), Stewart (2006), and Canaday (2008).
35. See Di Matteo (2012).
36. Ryan-Collins et al. (2017) note how Thomas Jefferson associated small-scale land ownership as a virtue and how in the twentieth century politicians have promoted home ownership as means of promoting democracy.
37. Card et al. (2004).
38. Data Source: OECD STAT Aug 23, 2017.

39. Source: Guardian Trade Union Database. https://www.theguardian.com/news/datablog/2010/apr/30/union-membership-data#data. For a discussion see Lewis (2010).
40. For an overview of Canadian labor history, see: http://www.thecanadianencyclopedia.ca/en/article/working-class-history/
41. See Riddell (1993).
42. Mayer (2004).
43. Riddell (1993), for the period 1920–1990, is union membership as a percentage of nonagricultural paid workers. The OECD numbers for 1980–2014 are from OECD STAT and are for union members as a percent share of wage and salary workers.
44. See Galarneau and Sohn (2013).
45. Intergenerational wealth transmission can have significant effects on wealth distribution over time. The simple decision as to whether inheritances go to the firstborn son (primogeniture) or whether there is more partible or equal division (multi-geniture) is important in affecting wealth distribution. See Di Matteo (2016a, b).
46. The role of inheritance is also noted in the research on pre-industrial European economic inequality being conducted by EINITE at Bocconi University and the work of scholars such as Alfani (2015), Alfani and Ryckbosch (2016), Alfani and Ammannati (2017), and Ryckbosch (2017).
47. Delong (2003: 4–5).
48. Ransom and Sutch (1986) argued that the nineteenth century saw America's move from a target bequest motive to life-cycle saving. Using evidence from surveys of industrial workers in Michigan and Maine, they found declining savings rates for older workers and a hump-shaped profile that would indicate life-cycle saving. Di Matteo (1997) using probate data also finds evidence of such a transition for the nineteenth century in Ontario. In the colonial United States, Alston and Schapiro (1984) argue the North was characterized by multi-geniture and the South primogeniture. Salmon (1980) finds that Germans in east-central Illinois used partible inheritance and the Irish impartible. Newell (1986) for Butler County, Ohio found more equal estate division over time. The British legal legacy in nineteenth century English Canada made primogeniture dominant, but there was a move toward greater equality in estate division. Gagan (1976) describes three inheritance systems in nineteenth-century Peel County, Ontario: partible, impartible, and partible-impartible. While the first two are self-explanatory, the last is whereby the estate was devolved on one or several heirs (usually males) with compensation payments to the siblings.
49. See The Economist (2017) 'Death of the death tax', November 25th to December 1st, 20–22.

50. The Canadian federal estate tax ended in 1973 as part of a process of tax reform, given that it was believed that the presence of both capital gains taxation at death and an estate tax amounted to double taxation.
51. Lee (1966) separates the forces affecting migration into pluses, minuses, and zeros, with pluses pulling individuals in, minuses pushing them out, and zeros with evenly balanced factors. See also King (2012) for an overview of migration models.

## References


Alfani, G. (2015). Economic Inequality in Northwestern Italy: A Long-Term View (Fourteenth to Eighteenth Centuries). *Journal of Economic History, 75*(4), 1058–1096.

Alfani, G., & Ammannati, F. (2017). Long-Term Trends in Economic Inequality: The Case of the Florentine State, c. 1300–1800. *The Economic History Review, 70*(4), 1072–1102.

Alfani, G., & Ryckbosch, W. (2016). Growing Apart in Early Modern Europe? A Comparison of Inequality Trends in Italy and the Low Countries, 1500–1800. *Explorations in Economic History, 62*, 1430153.

Alston, L. J., & Schapiro, M. O. (1984). Inheritance Laws Across Colonies: Causes and Consequences. *Journal of Economic History, 44*(2), 277–287.

Ando, A., & Modigliani, F. (1963). The 'Life-Cycle' Hypothesis of Saving: Aggregate Implications and Tests. *American Economic Review, 53*, 55–84.

Armour, P., Burkhauser, R. V., & Larrimore, J. (2013). Deconstructing Income Inequality Measures: A Crosswalk from Market Income to Comprehensive Income. *American Economic Review: Papers and Proceedings, 103*(3), 173–177.

Atack, J., & Bateman, F. (1981). Egalitarianism, Inequality, and Age: The Rural North in 1860. *Journal of Economic History, XLI*, 85–93.

Atkinson, A. B., & Brandolini, A. (2001). Promise and Pitfalls in the Use of "Secondary" Data-Sets: Income Inequality in OECD Countries as a Case Study. *Journal of Economic Literature, 39*(3), 771–799.

Barro, R. J. (2000). Inequality and Growth in a Panel of Countries. *Journal of Economic Growth, 5*, 5–32.

Barro, R. J. (2008). *Inequality and Growth Revisited*. ADB Working Paper on Regional Economic Integration No. 11.

Bernheim, B. D., Shleifer, A., & Summers, L. H. (1985). The Strategic Bequest Motive. *Journal of Political Economy, 93*(6), 1045–1076. https://doi.org/10.1086/261351.

Burkhauser, R. V., Hahn, M., & Wilkins, R. (2013). *Measuring Top Incomes Using Tax Record Data: A Cautionary Tale from Australia*. NBER Working Paper No. 19121.

Canaday, N. (2008). The Accumulation of Property by Southern Blacks and Whites: Individual-Level Evidence from a South Carolina Cotton County, 1910–1919. *Explorations in Economic History, 45*, 51–75.

Card, D., Lemieux, T., & Riddell, C. (2004). Unions and Wage Inequality. *Journal of Labour Research, 25*(4), 519–559.

Davies, J. B., & Shorrocks, A. F. (2000). The Distribution of Wealth. In A. B. Atkinson & F. Bourguignon (Eds.), *Handbook of Income Distribution* (Vol. 1, pp. 605–675). New York: Elsevier Science.

Deaton, A. (2013). *The Great Escape: Health, Wealth and the Origins of Inequality.* Princeton: Princeton University Press.

Deininger, K., & Squire, L. (1998). New Ways of Looking at Old Issues: Inequality and Growth. *Journal of Development Economics, 57*, 259–287.

Delong, B. (2003). Bequests: An Historical Perspective. In A. H. Munnell & A. Sundén (Eds.), *Death and Dollars: The Role of Gifts and Bequests in America, Chapter 2.* Washington, DC: Brookings Institution Press.

Di Matteo, L. (1997). The Determinants of Wealth and Asset Holding in Nineteenth Century Canada: Evidence from Micro-data. *Journal of Economic History, 57*(4), 907–934.

Di Matteo, L. (2001). Patterns and Determinants of Wealth Inequality in Late-Nineteenth Century Ontario. *Social Science History, 25*(3), 347–380.

Di Matteo, L. (2012). Land and Inequality in Canada 1870–1930. *Scandinavian Economic History Review, 60*(3), 309–334.

Di Matteo, L. (2013b). *Measuring Government in the 21st Century: An International Overview of the Size and Efficiency of Public Spending.* Vancouver: Fraser Institute.

Di Matteo, L. (2016a). Wealth Distribution and the Canadian Middle Class: Historical Evidence and Policy Implications. *Canadian Public Policy, 42*(2), 132–151.

Di Matteo, L. (2016b). All Equal in the Sight of God: Economic Inequality and Religion in the Early Twentieth Century. *European Review of Economic History, 20*, 23–45.

Di Matteo, L. (2017b). Major Changes to the Federal Personal Income Tax: 1917–2017. In W. Watson & J. Clemens (Eds.), *Zero to 50 in 100 Years: The History and Development of Canada's Personal Income Tax.* Vancouver: Fraser Institute.

Disney, R., & Luo, G. (2014). *The Right to Buy Public Housing in Britain: A Welfare Analysis* (Working paper W15/05). Institute for Fiscal Studies.

Dupont, B., & Rosenbloom, J. (2016, April). *The Impact of the Civil War on Southern Wealth Holders.* NBER Working Paper No. 22184.

de la Escosura, L. P. (2008). Inequality, Poverty and the Kuznets Curve in Spain, 1850–2000. *European Review of Economic History, 12*(3), 287–324.

Gagan, D. (1976). The Indivisibility of Land: A Micro-analysis of the System of Inheritance in Nineteenth Century Ontario. *Journal of Economic History, 36*, 126–141.

Galarneau, D., & Sohn, T. (2013). *Long-Term Trends in Unionization*. Statistics Canada, Insights on Canadian Society. 75-006-X. http://www.statcan.gc.ca/pub/75-006-x/2013001/article/11878-eng.pdf

Gallman, R. E. (1978). Professor Pessen on the 'Egalitarian Myth'. *Social Science History, 2*, 194–207.

Gallup, J. L. (2012). *Is There a Kuznets Curve?* Working Paper. https://www.pdx.edu/econ/sites/www.pdx.edu.econ/files/kuznets_complete.pdf

Green, A. G. (1967). Regional Aspects of Canada's Economic Growth, 1890–1929. *The Canadian Journal of Economics, 33*(2), 232–245.

Green, A. G. (1968). Regional Inequality, Structural Change, and Economic Growth in Canada. *Economic Development and Cultural Change, 17*, 567–583.

Green, A. G. (1971). *Regional Aspects of Canadian Economic Growth*. Toronto: University of Toronto Press.

Gregson, M. E. (1996). Wealth Accumulation and Distribution in the Midwest in the Late Nineteenth Century. *Explorations in Economic History, 33*, 524–538.

Higgins, M., & Williamson, J. G. (2002). Explaining Inequality the World Round: Cohort Size, Kuznets Curves, and Openness. *Southeast Asian Studies, 40*(3), 268–302. Reprinted in B. Milanovic (Ed.) (2012). *Globalization and Inequality*. Cheltenham: Elgar.

King, R. (2012). *Theories and Typologies of Migration: An Overview and A Primer*. Willy Brandt Working Papers in International Migration and Ethnic Relations, Malmo University, 3/12.

Kuznets, S. (1955). Economic Growth and Income Inequality. *American Economic Review, XLV*(1), 1–28.

Kuznets, S. (1966). *Modern Economic Growth Rate, Structure and Spread*. New Haven: Yale University Press.

Landy, B. (2013, August 28). *A Tale of Two Recoveries: Wealth Inequality After the Great Recession*. The Century Foundation. Issue Brief. https://tcf.org/content/commentary/a-tale-of-two-recoveries-wealth-inequality-after-the-great-recession/

Lee, E. S. (1966). A Theory of Migration. *Demography, 3*(1), 47–57.

Lemon, J. T. (1972). *The Best Poor Man's Country: A Geographical Study of Early Southeastern Pennsylvania*. Baltimore: John Hopkins Press.

Lewis, S. (2010, April 30). How Union Membership Has Grown—And Shrunk. *The Guardian*. https://www.theguardian.com/news/datablog/2010/apr/30/union-membership-data#data

Lindert, P. H. (1991). Toward a Comparative History of Income and Wealth. In Y. S. Brenner, H. Kaelble, & M. Thomas (Eds.), *Income Distribution in Historical Perspective* (pp. 212–231). Cambridge: Cambridge University Press.

Lindert, P. H., & Williamson, J. G. (1985). Growth, Equality and History. *Explorations in Economic History, 22*, 341–377.

Mayer, G. (2004). *Union Membership Trends in the United States. Congressional Research Service Report for Congress.* Cornell University ILR School, DigitalCommons@ILR.

Milanovic, B. (2016). *Global Inequality: A New Approach for the Age of Globalisation.* Cambridge, MA: Harvard University Press.

Modigliani, F. (1988a). Measuring the Contribution of Intergenerational Transfers to Total Wealth: Conceptual Issues and Empirical Findings. In D. Kessler & A. Masson (Eds.), *Modelling the Accumulation and Distribution of Wealth* (pp. 21–52). Oxford: Clarendon Press..

Modigliani, F. (1988b). The Role of Intergenerational Transfers and Life Cycle Saving in the Accumulation of Wealth. *Journal of Economic Perspectives, 2*(2), 15–40. https://doi.org/10.1257/jep.2.2.15.

Newell, W. H. (1986). Inheritance on the Maturing Frontier: Butler County Ohio, 1803–1865. In S. L. Engerman & R. E. Gallman (Eds.), *Long-Term Factors in American Economic Growth, NBER Studies in Income and Wealth* (Vol. 51, pp. 261–303). Chicago: University of Chicago Press.

Peacock, A. T., & Wiseman, J. (1967). *The Growth of Public Expenditure in the United Kingdom* (Vol. 1). London: Allen & Unwin.

Piketty, T. (2000). Theories of Persistent Inequality and Intergenerational Mobility. In A. B. Atkinson & F. Bourguignon (Eds.), *Handbook of Income Distribution* (Vol. I, pp. 429–476). New York: Elsevier Science.

Piketty, T. (2014). *Capital in the 21st Century.* Cambridge, MA: Harvard University Press.

Piketty, T., & Saez, E. (2013). A Theory of Optimal Inheritance Taxation. *Econometrica, 81*(5), 1851–1886.

Piketty, T., & Zucman, G. (2013). *Capital Is Back: Wealth-Income Ratios in Rich Countries, 1700–2010.* Working Paper, Paris School of Economics.

Piketty, T., Postel-Vinay, G., & Rosenthal, J.-L. (2006). Wealth Concentration in a Developing Economy: Paris and France, 1807–1994. *American Economic Review, 96*(1), 236–256.

Pikkety, T., Postel-Vinay, G., & Rosenthal, J.-L. (2014). Inherited vs Self-Made Wealth: Theory & Evidence from a Rentier Society (Paris 1872–1927). *Explorations in Economic History, 51*, 21–40.

Ransom, R. L., & Sutch, R. (1986). The Life-Cycle Transition: A Preliminary Report on Wealth-Holding in America, Chapter 10. In*Income and Wealth Distribution in Historical Perspective* (Vol. 1). Utrecht: Rijksuniversiteit te Utrecht, Two Volumes.

Riddell, C. (1993). Unionization in Canada and the United States: A Tale of Two Countries, Chapter 4. In D. Card & R. B. Freeman (Eds.), *Small Differences that Matter: Labor Markets and Income Maintenance in Canada and the United States* (pp. 109–148). Chicago: National Bureau of Economic Research, University of Chicago Press.

Rognlie, M. (2015). *Deciphering the Fall and Rise in the Net Capital Share: Accumulation on Scarcity?* Brookings Papers on Economic Activity, Spring, pp. 1–54.

Roine, J., & Waldenström, D. (2015). Long-Run Trends in the Distribution of Income and Wealth. In A. B. Atkinson & F. Bourguignon (Eds.), *Handbook of Income Distribution* (Vol. 2A, pp. 469–592). Amsterdam: Elsevier.

Royal Commission. (1979). *Royal Commission on the Distribution of Income and Wealth.* Report No. 7, Fourth Report on the Standing Reference. London: HMSO.

Ryan-Collins, J., Lloyd, T., & Macfarlane, L. (2017). *Rethinking the Economics of Land and Housing.* London: Zed Books.

Ryckbosch, W. (2017). Economic Inequality and Growth Before the Industrial Revolution: The Case of the Low Countries (Fourteenth to Nineteenth Centuries). *European Review of Economic History, 20*, 1–22.

Saez, E., & Veall, M. (2005). The Evolution of High Incomes in Northern America: Lessons from Canadian Evidence. *American Economic Review, 95*, 831–849.

Salmon, S. (1980). Ethnic Differences in Farm Family Land Transfers. *Rural Sociology, 45*, 290–308.

Savvidesa, A., & Stengos, T. (2000). Income Inequality and Economic Development: Evidence from the Threshold Regression Model. *Economics Letters, 69*, 207–212.

Scheidel, W. (2017a, February 21). The Only Thing, Historically, That's Curbed Inequality: Catastrophe. *The Atlantic.* https://www.theatlantic.com/business/archive/2017/02/scheidel-great-leveler-inequality-violence/517164/

Scheidel, W. (2017b). *The Great Leveler: Violence and the History of Inequality from the Stone Age to the Twenty-First Century.* Princeton: Princeton University Press.

Skott, P. (2011). *Increasing Inequality and Financial Instability.* Department of Economics Working Paper, University of Massachusetts, Amherst.

Statistics Canada. (2013). National Household Survey: Income and Housing – Homeownership and Shelter Costs in Canada, National Household Survey year 2011 (99-014-X). http://www12.statcan.gc.ca/nhs-enm/2011/assa/99-014-x/2011002/c-g/c-g01-eng.cfm

Stewart, J. I. (2006). Migration to the Agricultural Frontier and Wealth Accumulation, 1860–1870. *Explorations in Economic History, 43*(4), 547–577.

Stiglitz, J. (2012). *The Price of Inequality.* New York: W.W. Norton & Company.

Tanzi, V. (2011). *Government Versus Markets: The Changing Economic Role of the State.* Cambridge: Cambridge University Press.

The Economist Magazine. (2017). Death of the Death Tax. November 25th to December 1st, pp. 20–22.

Wagner, A. (1893). *Grundlegung der politischen Oekonomie: 1. Theil, Grundlagen der Volkswirthschaft*. Leipzig: CF Winter, 2 vols.
Wagner, A. (1894). *Grundlegung der politischen Oekonomie: 2. Theil, Volkswirthschaft und Recht, besonders Vermogensrecht*. Leipzig: CF Winter, 5 vols.
Williamson, J. G. (1965). Regional Inequality and the Process of National Development. *Economic Development and Cultural Change, 13*, 1–84, Part 2.
Williamson, J. G. (1996a). *Globalization and Inequality Then and Now: The Late 19th and Late 20th Centuries Compared*. National Bureau of Economic Research, Working Paper 5491.
Williamson, J. G. (1996b). Globalization, Convergence and History. *The Journal of Economic History, 56*(2), 277–306.
Williamson, J. G. (1998). Growth, Distribution and Demography: Some Lessons from History. *Explorations in Economic History, 35*(3), 241–271.
Williamson, J. G., & Lindert, P. H. (1980). *American Inequality: A Macroeconomic History*. New York: Academic Press.

CHAPTER 5

# Examining the Evidence: Wealth Inequality in the North Atlantic Anglosphere

**Abstract** Non-parametric smoothing reveals that wealth inequality was higher in the United Kingdom than the United States before industrialization, but American inequality grew to match the United Kingdom by the mid-nineteenth century. Industrialization does appear marked in all three Anglosphere countries by rising wealth inequality. Evidence for Canada, the United States, and the United Kingdom shows reduced wealth inequality starting in the twentieth century but a rebound in the United States near the end. Pooled regression models show key determinants of wealth inequality to be unionization rates, home ownership, housing policy, land policy, estate taxation, globalization, war, and also the source of data. As well, inequality in the United States and the United Kingdom is usually significantly higher than in Canada.

**Keywords** LOWESS • Regression • Significance

The available data compiled for Gini coefficients over time and the wealth share of the top 1 percent and the top 10 percent of the wealth distribution for Canada, the United States, and the United Kingdom are provided in Appendices 2, 3, and 4. While the recent preoccupation with the wealth share of the top 1 percent has dominated the discussion of wealth



L. Di Matteo, *The Evolution and Determinants of Wealth Inequality in the North Atlantic Anglo-Sphere, 1668–2013*,
https://doi.org/10.1007/978-3-319-89773-8_5

inequality, an effort is made to use measures other than only the top 1 percent wealth share. These measures are used because they provide a diversity of estimates and also because they are the measures most consistently available for both countries over the entire span of time from 1668 to 2013.

Modern studies of historic inequality are making efforts to construct new and consistent data series in an effort to examine wealth shares of the top 1 percent, but many of the studies from which historical inequality estimates in this survey are drawn rely on Gini coefficients, and the wealth shares of the top 1 or 10 percent are not always available on a consistent basis. The data sources vary considerably, and the range of the data often rarely extends into the past beyond the late nineteenth century.

As well, examining the wealth of the top 10 percent helps account for the fact that much of the wealth redistribution of the twentieth century away from the top 1 percent does appear to have also benefitted the top deciles of the wealth distribution—essentially, the next 9 percent or the upper middle classes—and the immediate next two deciles—whereas the wealth shares of the bottom 50 percent have changed little over time. Di Matteo (2016a) found that for Canada despite the onset of more redistributive government policies in the twentieth century, the wealth share of the bottom 50 percent has remained low over time, and this ultimately represents a more pressing set of policy and social concerns than the erosion of the middle class.

Reeves (2017) has argued that, in the United States, the rhetoric of economic inequality and its emphasis on pointing to the top 1 percent while assuming the other 99 percent are somehow all equally worse off ignores that fact that the upper middle class—the top fifth of wealth and income distributions—are actually also in very favored positions. Moreover, there is a culture of entitlement among the American upper middle class and a separation in wealth, attitude, education, and upbringing that via its *hoarding of opportunity* has also been a major factor in the growth of American wealth inequality. As a result, extending the inequality measures to include the top 10 percent is a way of partially addressing this.

It should also be noted that top shares of wealth or income are not always regarded as suitable inequality measures as they do not meet the Pigou-Dalton criteria. In brief, the Pigou-Dalton criteria maintain that an inequality measure should decrease as a consequence of any wealth transfer from a wealth receiver to another with a smaller level of wealth, which is not always the case with wealth shares.[1] Nonetheless, wealth shares are a commonly used measure in inequality studies because of their simplicity and convenience as very often they are the only measure available. On the other hand, the Gini coefficient can also be a problematic metric, as it does not properly reflect changes in the top tail of the distribution. The Gini can also be sensitive to changes in the middle of the distribution, which may be also driven by measurement errors rather than anything else.[2]

Table 5.1 presents a summary overview of average inequality by time period—for each country—for the three measures used in this study: Gini coefficient, wealth share of the top 1 percent, and wealth share of the top 10 percent. Pre-1850, the average value of the Gini coefficient for the United States was lower than the United Kingdom at 0.670 compared to 0.767—which could be attributed to greater relative land abundance and availability—especially during the colonial settlement period in the United States. However, by the latter half of the nineteenth century (1850–1900), the average value of the Gini coefficient was 0.831 for the United States

**Table 5.1** Average wealth inequality measures by time period

| | | **Gini** | |
|---|---|---|---|
| | *United Kingdom* | *United States* | *Canada* |
| Pre-1850 | 0.767 | 0.670 | NA |
| 1850–1900 | 0.840 | 0.831 | 0.676 |
| 1900–1950 | 0.863 | NA | 0.739 |
| 1950–1975 | 0.810 | 0.755 | 0.672 |
| 1975–2013 | 0.660 | 0.808 | 0.705 |
| | | **Top 1 percent wealth share (%)** | |
| | *United Kingdom* | *United States* | *Canada* |
| Pre-1850 | 24.7 | 23.5 | NA |
| 1850–1900 | 63.5 | 32.0 | 12.1 |
| 1900–1950 | 55.1 | 35.4 | 21.5 |
| 1950–1975 | 30.2 | 27.3 | 13.8 |
| 1975–2013 | 18.8 | 27.4 | 18.6 |
| | | **Top 10 percent wealth share (%)** | |
| | *United Kingdom* | *United States* | *Canada* |
| Pre-1850 | 70.5 | 55.7 | NA |
| 1850–1900 | 91.3 | 71.7 | 55.5 |
| 1900–1950 | 90.2 | 78.0 | 63.5 |
| 1950–1975 | 70.9 | 69.6 | 54.7 |
| 1975–2013 | 51.4 | 68.7 | 54.0 |

and 0.840 for the United Kingdom, reflecting rising inequality in both countries during the industrial age. For the nineteenth century, wealth inequality was higher in both the United States and the United Kingdom relative to Canada, which—for the period 1850 to 1900—sees a relatively more modest average Gini wealth coefficient of 0.676.

In the case of the wealth shares of the top 1 percent, for the United Kingdom, they rose from an average of 24.7 percent in the pre-1850 period to 63.5 percent for the 1850–1900 period. For the United States, the increase was from 23.5 to 32 percent. The top 1 percent shares of both the United States and the United Kingdom were higher than Canada, which averaged 12.1 percent. Similar patterns between the pre-1850 period and the late nineteenth century are also evident for the average wealth share of the top 10 percent. Most remarkably, the average share of wealth held by the top 10 percent of the wealth distribution in the second half of the nineteenth century was just over 90 percent in the United Kingdom, approximately 72 percent in the United States, and about 56 percent in Canada.

The twentieth century sees continued high inequality for all three countries in the first half but is followed by declines after 1950, with the steepest declines in wealth inequality in the United Kingdom. For the United Kingdom, the average Gini coefficient drops from 0.840 between 1850 and 1900, to reach 0.810 by 1950–1975, while the wealth share of the top 1 percent falls from 63.5 to 30.2 percent. For the United Kingdom, the decline continues into the 1975–2013 period, where the average Gini coefficient of wealth inequality falls to 0.660, and the wealth share of the top 1 percent reaches 18.8 percent.

Canada sees the average value of its Gini coefficients rise between 1850–1900 and then 1900–1950, before also dropping in the 1950–1975 period. However, the period between 1950–1975 and 1975–2013 actually sees an increase in average Canadian Gini Coefficients as well as the average shares of the top 1 percent, though the share of the top 10 percent across these periods declines slightly.

For the United States, the 1850–1900 period sees a Gini coefficient of 0.831, and by the 1950–1975 period, it averages 0.755, before rebounding to 0.808 in the 1975–2013 period. The average wealth share of the top 1 percent actually rises from 32 percent in the 1850–1900 period to 35.4 percent in the 1900–1950 period but then declines afterward, reaching 27.3 percent over the 1950–1975 period and staying approximately the same past 1975.

While these averages are convenient summaries of wealth inequality over time, they do not provide sufficient detail of trends over time. In the end, they are averages for broad time periods. For all three of these countries, period averages do not provide a full picture of trends over time due to both the presence of outliers and differential numbers of observations by time period. As a result, different techniques rather than simple point estimates are more useful to visualize trends.

Figures 5.1, 5.2, and 5.3 plot the Gini coefficients against time separately for each of the three countries using a non-parametric local polynomial smoother. Figures 5.4, 5.5, and 5.6 plot the wealth shares of the top 1 percent against time separately for each of the three countries, while Figs. 5.7, 5.8, and 5.9 plot the wealth shares of the top 10 percent. In all of these figures, a third-degree polynomial smoothing line is estimated to gauge the broad direction of inequality changes and see if they are generally in accord with the literature and studies to date—that is, an increase during the era of industrialization, followed by decreased wealth inequality during

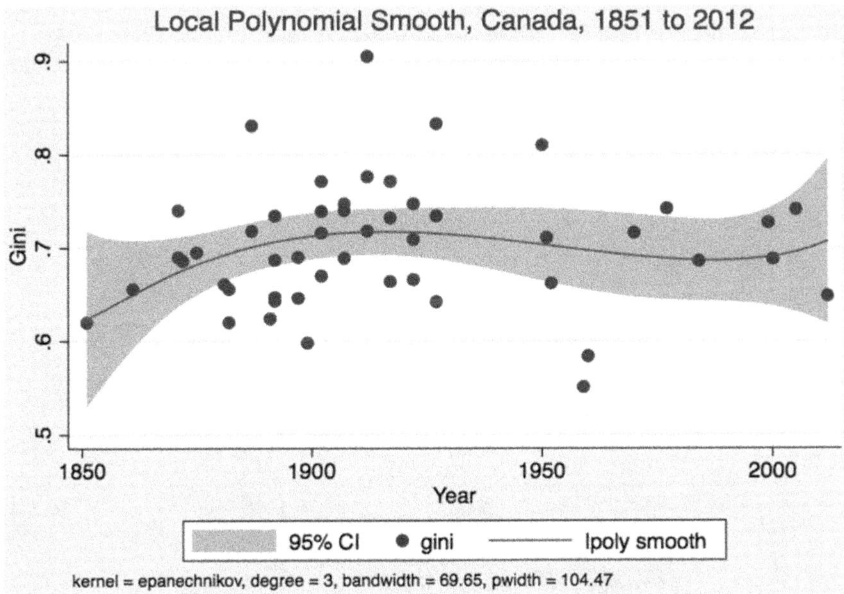


**Fig. 5.1** Gini coefficients of wealth inequality, Canada, 1851–2012

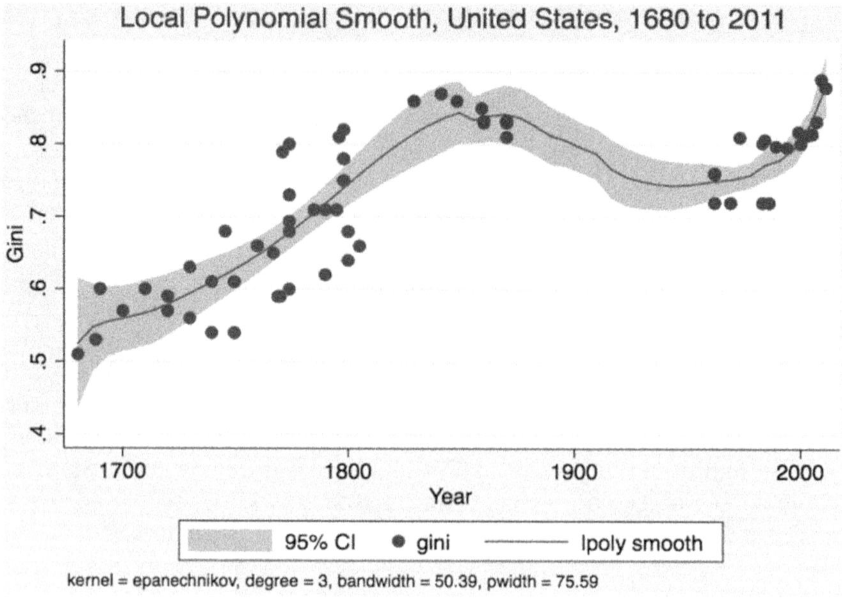


**Fig. 5.2** Gini coefficients of wealth inequality, United States, 1680–2011

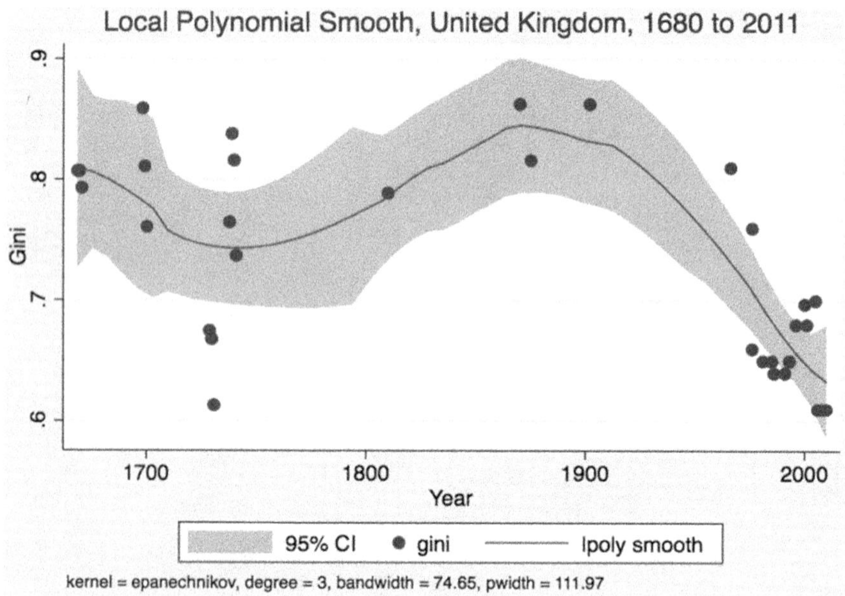


**Fig. 5.3** Gini coefficients of wealth inequality, United Kingdom, 1688–2010

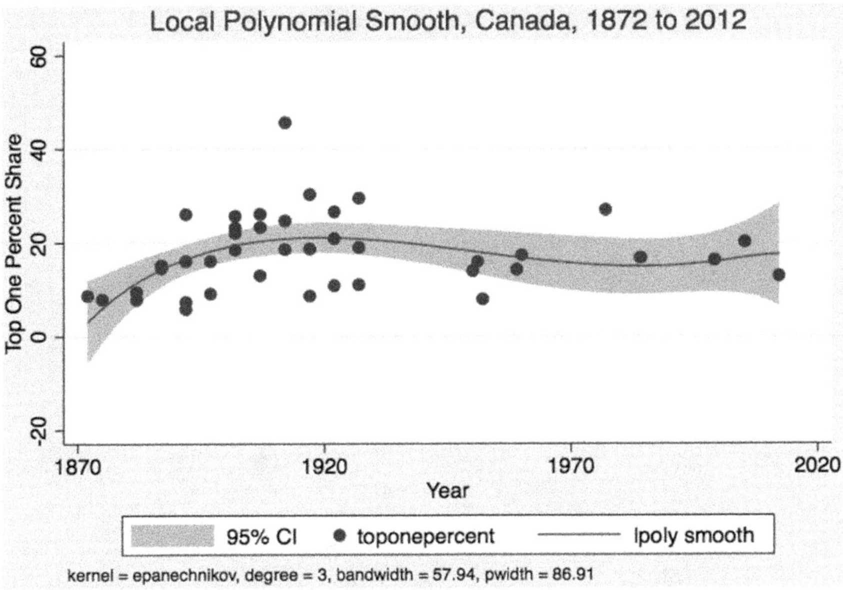


**Fig. 5.4** Wealth share (%) of the top 1 percent, Canada 1872–2012

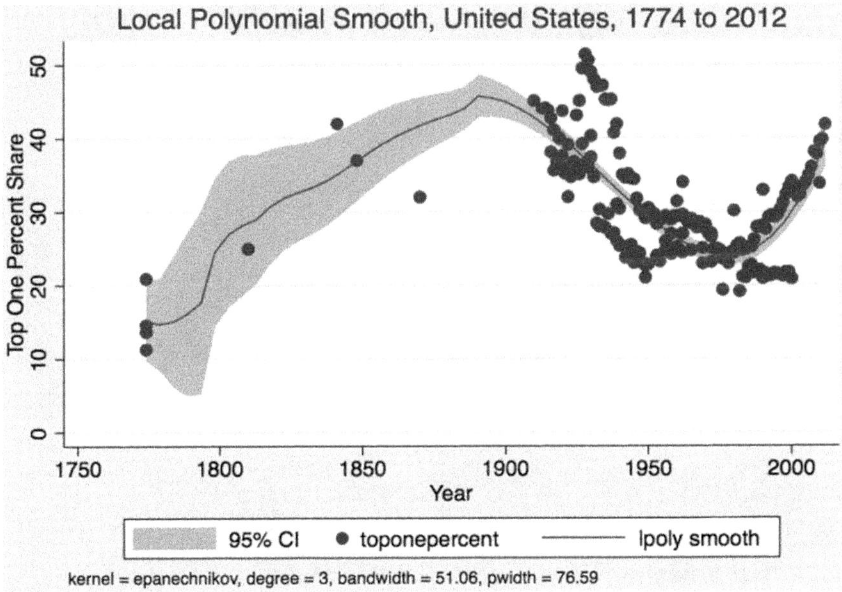


**Fig. 5.5** Wealth share (%) of the top 1 percent, United States, 1774–2012

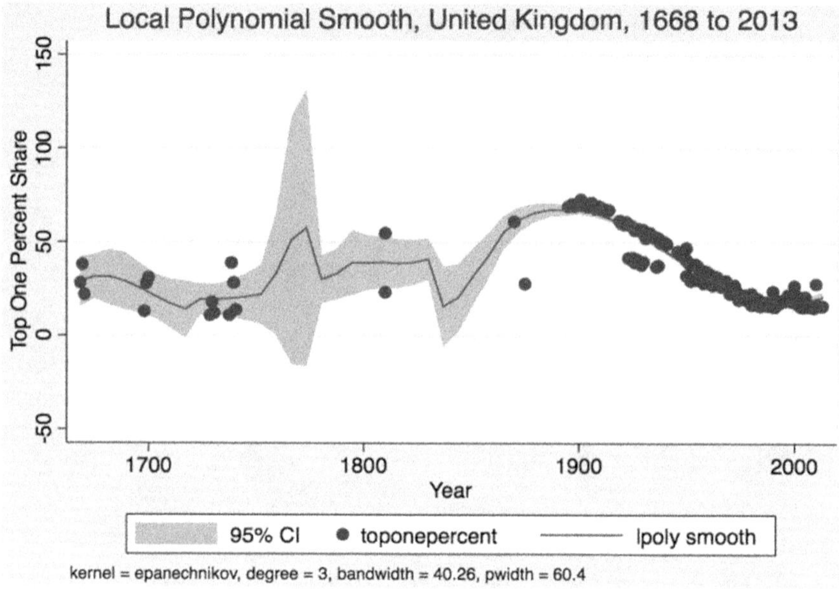


**Fig. 5.6** Wealth share (%) of the top 1 percent, United Kingdom, 1668–2013

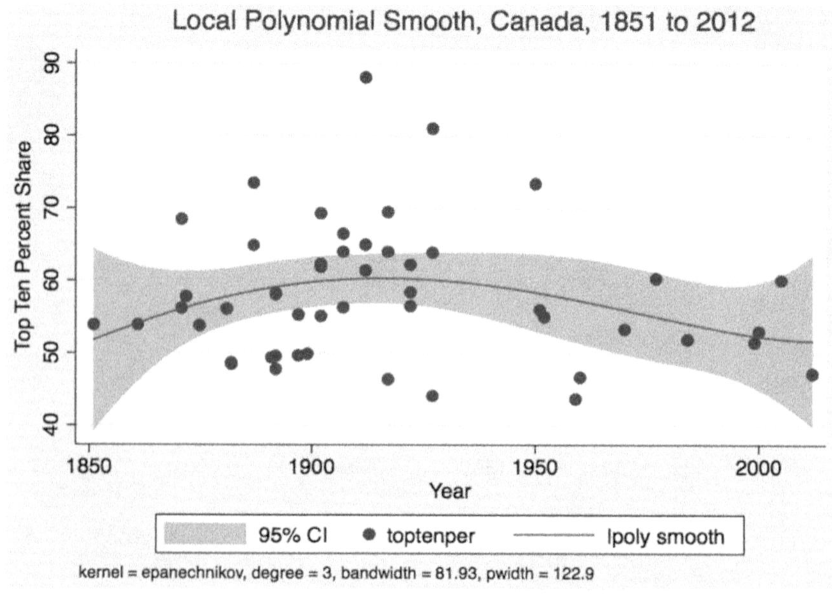


**Fig. 5.7** Wealth share (%) of the top 10 percent, Canada, 1851–2012

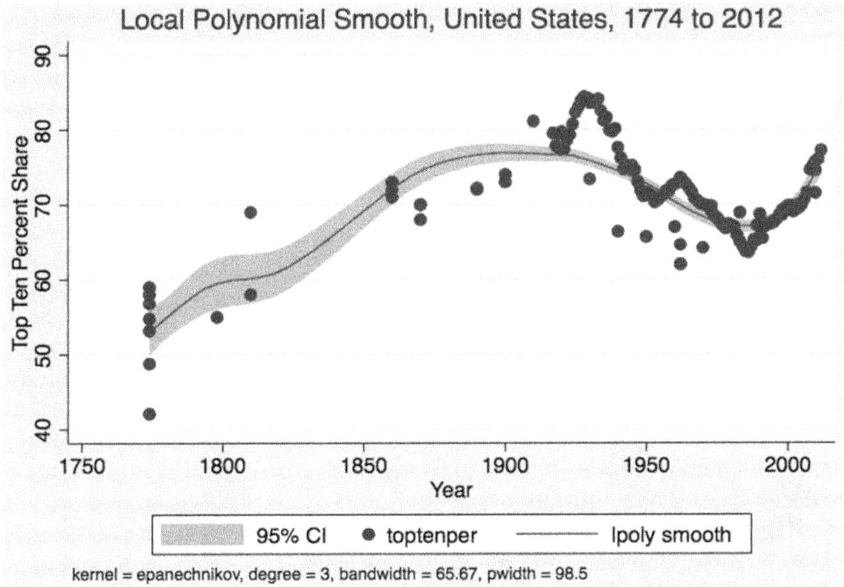


**Fig. 5.8** Wealth share (%) of the top 10 percent, United States, 1774–2012

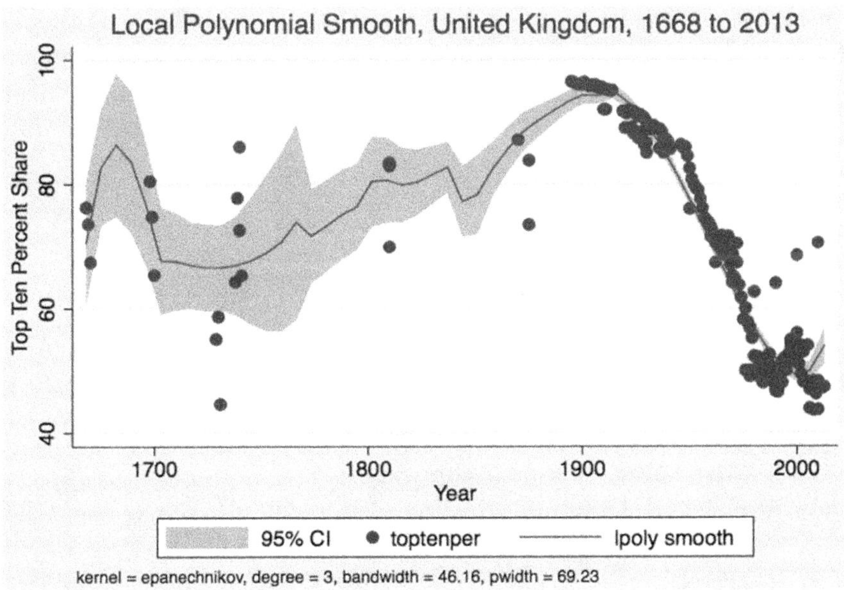


**Fig. 5.9** Wealth share (%) of the top 10 percent, United Kingdom, 1668–2013

the twentieth century.[3] Moreover, the visual technique is also a means whereby we can gauge if there has been an actual increase in wealth inequality since the last quarter of the twentieth century in these three countries.

The non-parametric smoothing technique is used to fit a trend line, as the technique does not assume a specific functional form and is not as sensitive to the presence of outliers as well as gaps in the data. All three wealth measures for each country exhibit time periods without substantial numbers of observations, making some type of interpolation helpful. This is also an important consideration in attempting to derive long-term trends from data that can be subject to extreme observations. Outliers are definitely a concern in the wealth data used here due to the combination of national and regional estimates in this data constructed using an assortment of techniques and data sets of varying size. The Canadian data in particular has some substantial variation, given the small size of some of the data sets used to construct some of the inequality estimates in years prior to 1930. The data for the United Kingdom and the United States also have some extreme values, particularly for the period prior to 1800.

As an example of differential results that can be obtained due in the absence of consistent data sources, there is the divergence in inequality measures for the United Kingdom since 1970—shown by David Giles with respect to the work of Thomas Piketty—that were highlighted in a Financial Times article.[4] While the trend over time in both series is about the same, the Giles estimates show an overall lower level of inequality than the Piketty numbers as a result of different estimates of wealth inequality from five sources of data that were used.

Data sources and availability are also an issue, as noted by Sutch (2017) in his critique of Piketty's data on the concentration of wealth in the United States. Sutch concludes that Piketty's data for the wealth share of the top 10 percent for the period 1870–1970 are unreliable, as the estimates are manufactured from the observations for the top 1 percent inflated by a constant 36 percentage points. According to Sutch, Piketty's data for the top 1 percent of the distribution for the nineteenth century (1810–1910) are also unreliable, as they are based on a single mid-century observation.

In terms of the smoothed trends, Figs. 5.1, 5.4, and 5.7 for Canada show rising inequality from the middle of the nineteenth century until the early twentieth century, then a slight decline until the 1970s, and then an increase, albeit small, into the twenty-first century—using the Gini coefficients and the top 1 percent share. However, for Canada, a decline in wealth inequality appears to persist after the 1970s when the wealth share of the top 10 percent is presented.

Overall, while still high, Canadian wealth inequality, as demonstrated by the polynomial smoothing, rises gently during the nineteenth century, does not demonstrate a great deal of fluctuation, and appears more stable over the long run—compared to the United States and the United Kingdom. Relatively lower levels of wealth inequality in Canada may be a function of the nature of the wealth accumulation and economic growth process. As noted, there is some evidence that more robust economic growth is correlated with more rapid growth in inequality, and Canadian economic growth during the nineteenth century after Confederation was especially slow until the vigorous growth performance of the wheat boom era started after 1896.[5]

When compared to the United States and the United Kingdom, average annual real GDP growth for Canada over the period 1870–2013 was actually higher at 3.9 percent, compared to 3.5 percent for the United States and 2.2 percent for the United Kingdom.[6] However, for the period 1870–1913, average annual real GDP growth was highest in the United States at 4.6 percent, compared to 4.2 percent for Canada and 1.9 percent for the United Kingdom. Meanwhile, for the period 1914–1945, real GDP growth rates in the United States averaged 4.1 percent, compared to 1.4 percent for the United Kingdom and 3.7 percent for Canada.

However, the relationship between higher wealth inequality and economic growth rates appears to break down somewhat after World War II. Over the period 1946–2013, real GDP growth in the United States averages 2.6 percent, compared to 2.8 percent in the United Kingdom and 3.7 percent in Canada. However, this is also a post-industrial period in all three countries, and it may be that higher economic growth must coincide with industrialization for it to have greater effects on raising wealth inequality.

For the United States, Figs. 5.2, 5.5, and 5.8 show a steep increase in wealth inequality from the colonial era until the late nineteenth century, which is then followed by some mitigation of that inequality into the twentieth century,[7] but then a substantial rebound in wealth inequality starting after 1970. Indeed, by the early twenty-first century, American wealth inequality is quite comparable to levels that were in existence toward the end of the late nineteenth century, whether one is looking at smoothed values of the Gini coefficient or the wealth shares of either the top 1 or 10 percent.

For the United Kingdom, Figs. 5.3, 5.6, and 5.9 reveal wealth inequality either declining or somewhat stable from the late seventeenth to the mid-eighteenth century, but there is then a steep ascent again until approximately 1900 followed by a steep decline into the twentieth century. The wealth share of the top 1 percent prior to 1850 does not appear to be increasing, but like the United States, there are relatively few data points for the top 1 percent prior to 1900 to confidently judge this. Unlike the United States and Canada, for the United Kingdom, the smoothed lines in Figs. 5.3, 5.6, or 5.9 do not appear to trend upward after the 1970s.

One point to note is that there may be boundary or edge effects when non-parametric estimates are done at the start or end of a time-series, which means any of these results at the start or tail end should be interpreted with caution.[8] However, in the case of the United Kingdom, this may also be a function of the data used given that the Piketty data generally shows higher levels of inequality for Britain than do other sources. As a result, Appendix 5 presents the polynomial smooth with the wealth shares of the top 10 percent that are 59 percent or less dropped, which places a stronger weight on the Piketty (2014) data for the period since 1970. The results show more of an upturn in wealth inequality as well as higher inequality generally in the present in this case but still not a major reversal.[9]

In a final effort to facilitate comparison, Figs. 5.10 and 5.11 first combine the Gini wealth inequality measures for all three countries in a time-series scatterplot and then provide separate LOWESS smooths[10] for each country alongside their original data points allowing for national-level differentiation. Meanwhile, Fig. 5.12 provides a LOWESS smooth of the top 1 percent for all three countries. Based on the LOWESS smooths of the Gini coefficients, the results show that American wealth inequality was less than that of the United Kingdom prior to 1800, whereas inequality in the United Kingdom was high and grew somewhat until the twentieth century. America was indeed a more egalitarian land relative to Britain during the colonial era, which no doubt helped spawn and perpetuate its ethos as a land of opportunity and plenty.[11] However, wealth distributions grew more unequal over time, and American wealth inequality also grew substantially between the mid-seventeenth and late nineteenth centuries.

When the LOWESS smooths of the top 1 percent are examined, they show American inequality below that of British, but both rise steeply and then both start to decline after 1900, with British inequality falling below that of the United States in the post-World War II era. The wealth share of the top 1 percent in the United States starts to rise after the mid-1970s and is nearly greater than that for the year 1900, as the twenty-first century

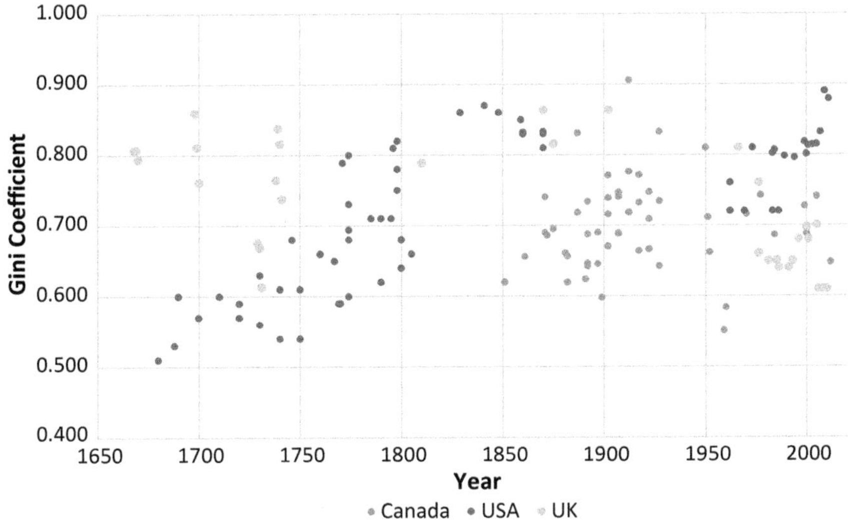


**Fig. 5.10** Gini coefficients by country: Canada, the United States, and the United Kingdom, 1680–2012

opens. Also of interest is the stabilization and then slight rise in the wealth share of the Canadian top 1 percent after the 1950s, following the modest decline of the first half of the twentieth century. The wealth share of the top 1 percent in Canada was generally lower than either the United Kingdom or the United States, though after the mid-1970s, Canada eventually becomes on par with the United Kingdom. Again, this emphasizes that rising wealth inequality in the late twentieth century has tended to be more of a North American than European phenomenon.

It is also useful to provide some comparison of the trends and patterns of inequality in these three Anglosphere countries to other European countries. Figure 5.13 uses data for the wealth share of the top 10 percent for six European countries obtained from Roine and Waldenström (2015), which spans the years 1789–2011 and estimates LOWESS smooths. The results for Denmark, Finland, France, Sweden, Switzerland, and Norway also show declining wealth inequality into the course of the twentieth century. Of these six European countries, only Denmark appears to be marked by an upsurge toward the end of the twentieth century, though the limited number of data points makes that a somewhat tentative observation.

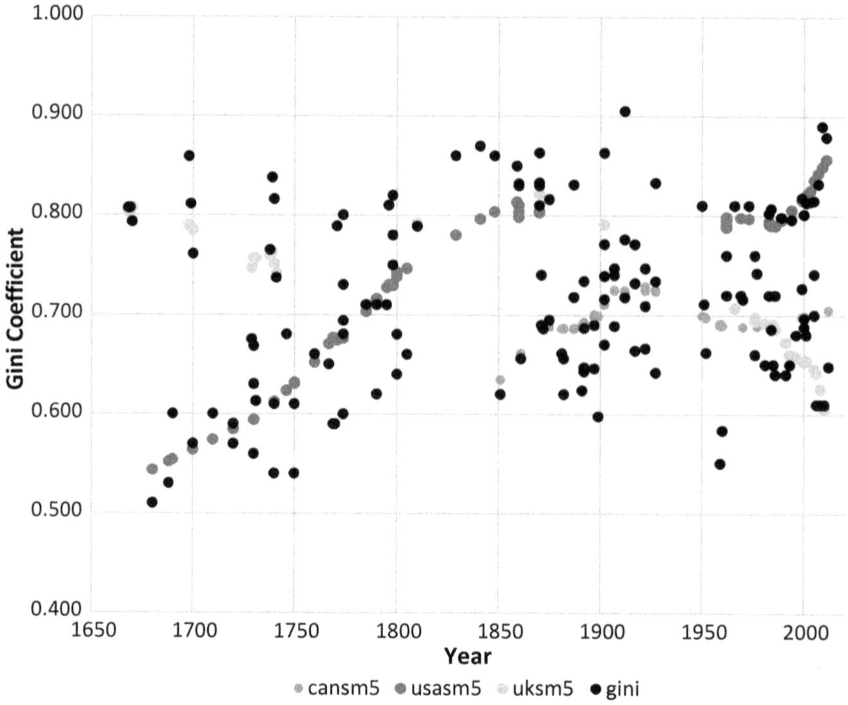


**Fig. 5.11** Gini coefficients by country with separate LOWESS smooth (bandwidth = 0.5): Canada, the United States, and the United Kingdom, 1680–2012

Of the three Anglosphere countries, it is the United Kingdom whose inequality trend most closely mirrors that of the European countries. Indeed, the United Kingdom, Norway, Sweden, and Finland appear to have all tracked along a similar path. Canada's wealth share for the top 10 percent is closer to France than the other Nordic countries even though it is sometimes referred to as the 'Scandinavia' of North America, given its perceived greater infrastructure of social programs relative to the United States including a single payer public health care system.[12] Nevertheless, both the United Kingdom and Canada diverge substantially from the United States, which displays the most overt trend toward greater wealth inequality during the period since the 1960s.

All three North Atlantic Anglosphere countries appear to be marked by rising inequality during nineteenth-century industrialization era followed

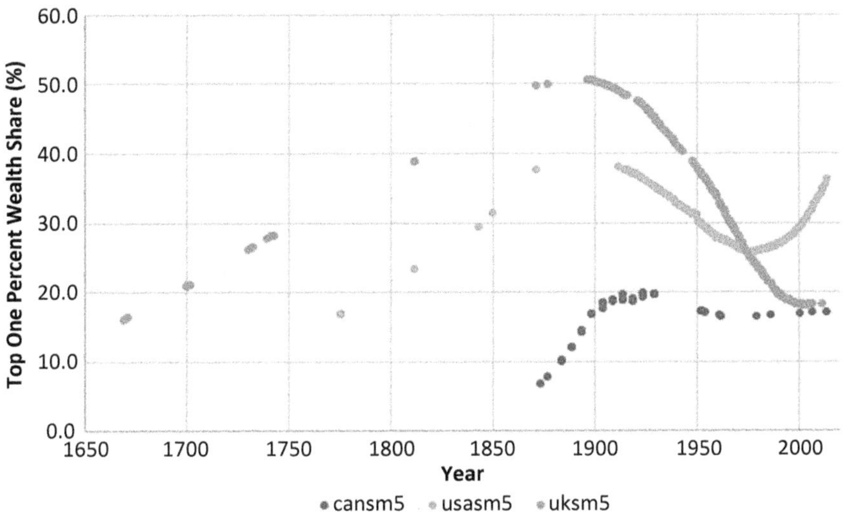


**Fig. 5.12** LOWESS smooth (bandwidth = 0.5) of wealth share (%) of the top 1 percent: Canada, United States, and United Kingdom. (Data sources: Same as those for Appendices 1, 2, and 3 and also Chartbook of Economic Inequality. http://www.chartbookofeconomicinequality.com/)

by declines in inequality during the twentieth century that bottomed out during the 1970s. Since the 1970s, there was at best a very modest increase in wealth inequality in Canada but a much more pronounced one in the United States. Interestingly enough, while it is still a very unequal society in terms of the level of inequality measured using the Gini coefficient or the top 10 percent share, inequality into the twenty-first century now appears to be lower in the United Kingdom than Canada or the United States.

One possible reason for this may be the result of changes to British housing markets that began in the 1980s and their potential effect on wealth distribution. Substantial numbers of rent subsidized council homes had been constructed in the wake of World War II as a result of the large-scale destruction of housing stock, and over time, governments began to emphasize home ownership as a means of distributing wealth more widely. As a result, in the United Kingdom, growth in home ownership saw the proportion of homeowners equaling that of renters by the early 1970s.

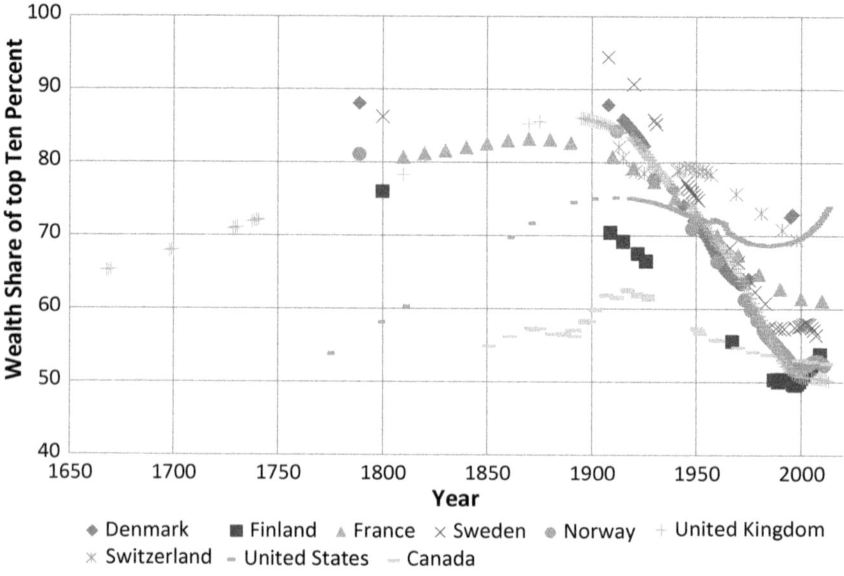


**Fig. 5.13** LOWESS smooth (bandwidth 0.8) of wealth share (%) of top 10 percent for selected countries: 1660–2013. (Data sources: Author's data and Roine and Waldenström (2014, 2015).

Indeed, some Conservative local authorities began to see their council housing stock not only as a burden on local taxpayers (subsidized rents and maintenance costs) but also as a potential means of widening asset ownership in their local communities, with a potential for positive social spillovers that might emanate from what was viewed as a more diverse social and economic mix of residents.[13] Under Margaret Thatcher in the 1980s, there were some significant changes that affected the British housing market—known as *Right to Buy* policies.

Under the Housing Act of 1980, there were incentives provided to public housing or council house tenants, which enabled them to buy their homes at a discount. In 1979, approximately 32 percent of all dwellings in Britain were council homes for a total of approximately 6.5 million properties. By 1987, over one million council houses and flats were sold, and by the mid-2000s, 2.8 million council homes had been sold in the United Kingdom. Indeed, the home ownership share was raised by about 15 percentage points—from 55 percent in 1979 to over 70 percent by the early 2000s.[14] This was a remarkable transition in the United Kingdom given that it had been largely a nation of renters. One can certainly hypothesize that rising home ownership rates may have had an impact on wealth distribution in the United Kingdom.

When an examination of these trends is combined with the discussion of inequality determinants and the push-pull framework discussed earlier, the next step is to see what the actual quantitative impact and significance of some of these factors might be. To measure the impact of determinants of wealth inequality over the long term in these three countries, simple regression analysis is employed, with Ordinary Least Squares (OLS) used as the estimation technique.[15]

Pooled regressions[16] for the determinants of inequality were specified that regress the natural log of the Gini coefficient, the natural log of the top 1 percent, and the natural log of the wealth share of the top 10 percent for these three countries, on a set of determinant variables that can either push up or pull down inequality.[17] These variables include year, year squared, and year cubed, in an effort to gauge the trend in wealth inequality over time, after accounting for other variables. As well, a dummy variable is specified taking on a value of 1 for the existence of a higher tax rate estate tax regime and 0 otherwise. The periods of higher estate tax regimes are defined as follows: for Canada, 1941–1973; for the United States, 1916–1977; and for the United Kingdom, 1894–1981. The estate tax variable is interacted with each of the three countries to obtain country specific results for the impact of estate taxation.

Furthermore, to take land abundance into account, a dummy variable is constructed for the period during which land grant programs were in existence in both the Canadian and American west. For Canada, this takes on a value of 1 for the years 1872–1930[18] (0 otherwise), which are the years during which the Federal Dominion Lands Act was in effect and which saw 1.25 million homesteads covering 80 million hectares made available.[19] For the United States, there were a number of homestead acts, but the main one was the Homestead Act of 1862, which was applied to public land in the American west. This variable takes on a value of 1 between 1862 and 1890—the year in which the superintendent of the US census announced that the Western frontier was closed.[20]

In addition, the effect of economic shocks that might affect inequality is captured via dummy variables that account for periods of major global war as indicated by major spikes in global conflict deaths since 1400: there are the War of Spanish Succession (1701–1713), Seven Years' War (1755–1763), Napoleonic Wars (1803–1815), World War I (1914–1918), and World War II (1939–1945).[21] As well, globalization is taken into account using two dummy variables for the eras of great trade and economic liberalization—the First Great Globalization (1870–1913) and the Second Great Globalization (1990–2009).

The period of the first globalization is generally seen as the 40 to 60-year time span prior to World War I, which was marked by new transportation and communication technologies such as steamships and the telegraph, migration of capital and labor, the spread of free market policies, and the adoption of the Gold Standard. This period is generally seen as ending with the start of World War I and the start of a period of deglobalization that saw higher tariff barriers and reduced trade flows. The period after World War II is often seen as the start of a new globalization era, given the movement to liberalize trade under the General Agreement on Trade and Tariffs (GATT), but it picks up speed with the fall of the Berlin Wall in 1990 and effectively slows down with the financial crisis and Great Recession of 2008–2009.[22]

The effect of the high economic growth of the post-World War II war economy and baby boom (1946–1973) is also taken into consideration with a separate dummy variable for the period. As well, a specific United Kingdom housing variable to capture the effect of the Housing Act of 1980 is constructed that takes on a value of 1 after 1980 and 0 otherwise. The inclusion of this variable actually marks one of the few empirical attempts to capture the economic effects of the 1980 Housing Act.[23] As well, a housing ownership variable was constructed for all three countries that took on a value of 1 if the homeownership rate was greater than 66 percent, and 0 otherwise, to see if very high rates of home ownership either raise or lower inequality.[24]

Additional dummy variables were also constructed to take into account the dynamics and effects of unionization trends in the three countries. For Canada and the United Kingdom—which had higher unionization rates than the United States—the peak unionization dummy variable took on a value of 1 when unionization rates for wage and salary workers were approximately 30 percent or higher, 0 otherwise. For the United States, a value of 1 when unionization rates were approximately 25 percent or higher, and 0 otherwise was used. For Canada, these were the years running from 1950 to 1996. For the United States, these years were from 1945 to 1965. For the United Kingdom, these were the years from 1918 to 1924 and 1942 to 1996.

Finally, dummy variables for the United States and the United Kingdom with Canada as the omitted category are included to allow for any other national fixed effects and comparisons after controlling for all other confounding factors. While these three countries share many commonalities, there are nonetheless some geographic, social, and cultural differences between them that may affect wealth inequality.[25] In addition, variables were also constructed to control for the data source used to construct the inequality measure, in an effort to see if the use of any particular data source affected measured inequality after controlling for other variables. These variables are survey data, probate records, tax data (defined as income tax and estate data), and all other sources (including census, income flow accounts, national balance sheets, and approaches using a combination of sources).[26]

STATA 15 was the statistics package used to estimate the regressions. Table 5.2 presents un-weighted OLS estimates, whereas Table 5.3 presented weighted OLS estimates, with the weighting variable being the country's population share.[27] This weighting procedure puts a heavier weight on observations associated with larger population shares, effectively putting a greater weight on observations from the United Kingdom and the United States.[28] Whereas the United Kingdom was initially the dominant country in terms of population size, during the late nineteenth century, the United States grew to become larger.

The un-weighted results for all three inequality measures show a high degree of significance (at the 5 percent level) for the individual coefficients, as well as a relatively high overall fit based on the adjusted r-squared. For the Gini coefficient regression, about 50 percent of the variation in inequality is explained by the regression, while for the share of the top 1 and 10 percent, the variation explained is higher at 69 and 78 percent respectively. For the weighted results, the corresponding figures for the adjusted r-squared are 44, 63, and 73 percent.

For both the weighted and un-weighted results and for both the Gini coefficient and the top 10 percent wealth share, the time variables show a significant cubic pattern, but the magnitude of the coefficients particularly for the weighted results suggests that wealth inequality generally rose since the 1660s and has continued rising well into the present but with some slowdown in rates of increase over the long term. For the top 1 percent, the un-weighted results show no significant trend over time, while for the weighted results, only the year squared and cubed variables are significant with their sign matching the other regressions.

**Table 5.2** OLS regression results: unweighted. Dependent variable: natural log of Gini coefficient and natural log of wealth share of top 1 and 10 percent

| | *Log of Gini* | | *Log of top 1 percent* | | *Log of top 10 percent* | |
|---|---|---|---|---|---|---|
| | *Coefficient* | *t-statistic* | *Coefficient* | *t-statistic* | *Coefficient* | *t-statistic* |
| ***Year*** | −0.0947 | **−3.18** | 0.0143 | 0.31 | −1.3061 | **−9.55** |
| ***Year Squared*** | 0.0001 | **3.40** | 0.0000 | 0.52 | 0.0007 | **9.70** |
| ***Year Cubed*** | 0.0000 | **−3.56** | 0.0000 | −1.43 | 0.0000 | **−9.84** |
| ***United States*** | 0.0649 | *1.87* | 0.5096 | *1.80* | 0.2849 | **9.34** |
| ***United Kingdom*** | 0.2780 | **7.35** | 0.8926 | **3.00** | 0.4489 | **11.67** |
| ***Canada Higher Estate Tax Regime*** | −0.1734 | −1.40 | −0.4611 | *−1.83* | −0.2061 | **−2.40** |
| ***US Higher Estate Tax Regime*** | −0.1585 | −1.31 | 0.0055 | 0.09 | −0.0366 | −1.25 |
| ***UK Higher Estate Tax Regime*** | −0.3423 | **−4.04** | −0.0684 | −0.70 | −0.0812 | **−2.13** |
| ***UK Housing Act*** | −0.5091 | **−6.44** | −0.4771 | **−4.82** | −0.2533 | **−6.33** |
| ***Global War*** | −0.0706 | *−1.86* | −0.0467 | −0.93 | −0.0077 | −0.32 |
| ***First Globalization Era*** | −0.0341 | −1.05 | 0.0853 | 1.47 | 0.0062 | 0.29 |
| ***Second Globalization Era*** | 0.0836 | *1.70* | 0.0761 | 1.24 | 0.0527 | **2.15** |
| ***Post-World War II Economic Boom*** | 0.1013 | 0.91 | −0.0442 | −0.93 | 0.0264 | 1.30 |
| ***Canadian Land Policy*** | 0.0299 | 0.85 | 0.7287 | **2.28** | −0.0174 | −0.77 |
| ***US Land Policy*** | 0.0943 | 1.42 | −0.2490 | −0.93 | −0.0648 | −1.10 |
| ***UK Unionization Rate >30%*** | −0.0372 | −0.56 | −0.2137 | **−4.49** | −0.1547 | **−8.42** |
| ***US Unionization Rate >25%*** | 0.0567 | 1.30 | −0.0781 | −1.35 | −0.0792 | **−2.74** |
| ***Canadian Unionization Rate >30%*** | −0.0891 | *−1.82* | 0.1756 | 0.57 | 0.1170 | 1.50 |

| | | | | | | |
|---|---|---|---|---|---|---|
| ***Survey Data*** | −0.0870 | ***−1.94*** | 0.4402 | **2.84** | 0.0532 | 1.60 |
| ***Tax Data*** | −0.0219 | −0.52 | 0.2673 | **3.09** | 0.0784 | **2.95** |
| ***Probate Records*** | −0.0351 | −1.26 | −0.9830 | **−6.18** | 0.0143 | 0.36 |
| ***US Homeownership Rate >66%*** | −0.0024 | −0.04 | 0.3466 | **4.56** | 0.2096 | **6.68** |
| ***UK Homeownership Rate >66%*** | 0.0000 | 0.00 | 0.0351 | 0.43 | 0.0087 | 0.28 |
| ***Canadian Homeownership Rate >66%*** | −0.1285 | ***−1.69*** | 0.0940 | 0.31 | 0.2860 | **3.55** |
| ***Constant*** | 53.7607 | **2.88** | −27.1172 | −0.90 | 792.7262 | **9.45** |
| n | 148 | | 438 | | 397 | |
| F(24, 123) | 7.04 | | | | | |
| F(24, 413) | | | 40.73 | | | |
| F(24, 372) | | | | | 59.33 | |
| Adjusted-R squared | 0.4964 | | 0.6857 | | 0.7795 | |

**Bold** Significant at 5 percent level

***Bold italic*** Significant at 10 percent level

**Table 5.3** OLS regression results: weighted by population share. Dependent variable: natural log of Gini coefficient and natural log of wealth share of top 1 and 10 percent

| | *Log of Gini* | | *Log of top 1 percent* | | *Log of top 10 percent* | |
|---|---|---|---|---|---|---|
| | *Coefficient* | *t-statistic* | *Coefficient* | *t-statistic* | *Coefficient* | *t-statistic* |
| ***Year*** | −0.1256 | **−4.47** | −0.0516 | −1.30 | −0.8811 | **−8.02** |
| ***Year Squared*** | 0.0001 | **4.38** | 0.0000 | *1.81* | 0.0005 | **8.11** |
| ***Year Cubed*** | 0.0000 | **−4.20** | 0.0000 | **−2.38** | 0.0000 | **−8.21** |
| ***United States*** | 0.0635 | 1.29 | 0.5102 | 0.96 | 0.2180 | **5.06** |
| ***United Kingdom*** | 0.2288 | **4.78** | 0.8149 | 1.51 | 0.4093 | **8.52** |
| ***Canada Higher Estate Tax Regime*** | −0.2410 | −1.42 | −0.3736 | −0.83 | −0.1561 | −0.98 |
| ***US Higher Estate Tax Regime*** | −0.1471 | −1.05 | 0.0567 | 1.22 | −0.0289 | −1.25 |
| ***UK Higher Estate Tax Regime*** | −0.3587 | **−3.45** | 0.0164 | 0.15 | −0.0957 | **−2.55** |
| ***UK Housing Act*** | −0.5581 | **−5.52** | −0.4994 | **−4.39** | −0.3392 | **−8.40** |
| ***Global War*** | −0.0695 | *−1.67* | −0.0563 | −1.43 | −0.0070 | −0.36 |
| ***First Globalization Era*** | −0.0540 | −1.04 | 0.2811 | **4.46** | 0.0301 | 1.29 |
| ***Second Globalization Era*** | 0.0197 | 0.49 | 0.0174 | 0.36 | 0.0067 | 0.36 |
| ***Post-World War II Economic Boom*** | 0.1055 | 0.77 | −0.0872 | **−1.96** | −0.0038 | −0.20 |
| ***Canadian Land Policy*** | 0.0437 | 0.68 | 0.7501 | 1.35 | 0.0107 | 0.56 |
| ***US Land Policy*** | 0.1115 | *1.65* | −0.4007 | *−1.87* | −0.0920 | *−1.82* |
| ***UK Unionization Rate >30%*** | −0.0062 | −0.07 | −0.1576 | **−2.80** | −0.1368 | **−6.53** |
| ***US Unionization Rate >25%*** | 0.0384 | 1.18 | −0.0669 | −1.50 | −0.0484 | **−2.37** |
| ***Canadian Unionization Rate >30%*** | −0.0841 | −1.00 | 0.1587 | 0.25 | 0.0404 | 0.28 |

| | | | | | | |
|---|---|---|---|---|---|---|
| ***Survey Data*** | −0.1641 | **−2.55** | 0.3803 | **3.52** | 0.0421 | 1.26 |
| ***Tax Data*** | 0.0101 | 0.16 | 0.2102 | **3.26** | 0.0846 | **2.74** |
| ***Probate Records*** | −0.0381 | −1.33 | −1.0990 | **−7.60** | −0.0691 | ***−1.62*** |
| ***US Homeownership Rate >66%*** | 0.0276 | 0.64 | 0.3245 | **6.08** | 0.1731 | **7.84** |
| ***UK Homeownership Rate >66%*** | 0.0322 | 0.41 | 0.0905 | 0.91 | 0.0366 | 1.06 |
| ***Canadian Homeownership Rate >66%*** | −0.2092 | −1.52 | 0.0278 | 0.04 | 0.1668 | 1.19 |
| ***Constant*** | 77.2393 | **4.46** | 25.4044 | 1.00 | 534.6767 | **7.98** |
| n | 148 | | 438 | | 397 | |
| F(24, 123) | 5.80 | | | | | |
| F(24, 413) | | | 32.35 | | | |
| F(24, 372) | | | | | 46.27 | |
| Adjusted-R squared | 0.4394 | | 0.6326 | | 0.7329 | |

**Bold** Significant at 5 percent level

***Bold italic*** Significant at 10 percent level

The more general lack of significance of the time variables with respect to the share of the top 1 percent suggests their wealth share has been the most invariant to time trends. For the Gini coefficient and the top 10 percent, these results suggest that the trend over time, all other things given, is toward greater wealth inequality, but fluctuations around this trend occur based on the effects of other determinants. These results also imply that the long-term effect of economic development, growth, and industrialization has been to increase wealth inequality, given that industrialization has particularly marked the years since 1750.

All other things given, inequality in the United States and the United Kingdom is usually significantly higher than in Canada but not always. In the un-weighted regressions, both the United States and the United Kingdom are always significantly higher than Canada. In the weighted regressions, the United Kingdom is significantly higher with respect to the Gini coefficient, while both the United States and the United Kingdom are higher than Canada using the top 10 percent but neither is with the top 1 percent.

Given the log-linear specification, the Gini coefficients from the un-weighted OLS regression are just over 6 percent higher for the United States and 28 percent higher for the United Kingdom. In the weighted regression case, only the United Kingdom is significantly higher at 23 percent. In the case of the wealth shares of the top 10 percent from the un-weighted results, they are 28 percent higher for the United States and 45 percent higher for the United Kingdom. The weighted results are 22 and 41 percent higher respectively.

However, when it comes to the wealth share of the top 1 percent, the United States is 51 percent and the United Kingdom 89 percent higher than Canada in the un-weighted results. For the weighted results, the corresponding difference is 51 percent for the United States and 81 percent for the United Kingdom, but these results are not significantly different from Canada. Nevertheless, it would appear that while Canada is marked by greater wealth equality relative to the United States and the United Kingdom when it comes to the Gini and top 10 percent wealth share, its top 1 percent may have a greater grip on wealth controlling for all other factors, given the lack of significant difference with either the Americans or the British once population size is taken into account.

With respect to the impact of periods of estate taxation, the results suggest that estate taxation did have some effect in depressing wealth inequality, but the results were most important for the United Kingdom and

Canada. With respect to the un-weighted results, Gini coefficients were significantly lower for the United Kingdom during its estate tax period, whereas the wealth shares of the top 10 percent were significantly lower for both Canada and the United Kingdom. The estate tax seems to have been significant in reducing the wealth share of the top 1 percent in Canada.

For Canada, the un-weighted results show estate taxation was associated with a 21 percent drop in inequality as measured by the wealth share of the top 10 percent and a 46 percent drop in the share of the top 1 percent. For the United Kingdom, the reductions were 34 percent for the Gini coefficient and 8 percent for the wealth share of the top 10 percent. As for the population share weighted results, the depressive effect of estate taxation on inequality was only significant for the United Kingdom, with a 36 percent reduction in inequality as measured by the Gini coefficient, and a 10 percent reduction in the wealth share of the top 10 percent. Moreover, the effect of estate taxation on the wealth share of the top 1 percent was not significant for any of the three countries. Taken together, these results suggest that estate taxation appears to have had some effect on reducing wealth inequality, but with perhaps the exception of Canada's wealth elite, the top 1 percent of the distribution were largely spared its effects.

In addition, the United Kingdom Housing Act Coefficient appears to have had a negative and significant effect reducing measures of Gini wealth inequality in the United Kingdom in the un-weighted regression by about 51 percent, the share of the top 1 percent by 48 percent, and the share of the top 10 percent by about 25 percent—all other things given. In the weighted regressions, the reductions ranged from 56 to 34 percent respectively. Quite interestingly, the United Kingdom Housing Act does appear to have affected the wealth share of even the top 1 percent in the United Kingdom with a nearly 50 percent drop in inequality for both the weighted and un-weighted regressions. Given its significance and size relative to the coefficients on estate taxation, the results suggest that the United Kingdom Housing Act was probably a more important factor in reducing wealth inequality than the estate tax.

Taken together, these results suggest that policy-induced mitigation of inequality via estate taxation did not occur in the United States but might have been of some consequence in Canada as well as the United Kingdom. Moreover, the Housing Act does appear to have been a factor in promoting greater equality of wealth distribution in the United Kingdom. However, with the exception of estate taxation in Canada and the Housing Act in the United Kingdom, policy efforts like estate taxation appear to have been of little consequence in affecting the wealth share of the top 1 percent of the wealth distribution in the United States.

Periods of global war were not a statistically significant factor in reducing wealth inequality when the share of the top 1 or 10 percent is examined. In the case of Gini coefficients, however, global war appears to have exhibited a negative effect on wealth inequality in both the weighted and un-weighted regressions in the range of a 7 percent reduction but with the results only significant at the 10 percent level.

The economic liberalization and economic growth of the two globalization eras does appear to have been a factor in increasing wealth inequality, particularly with respect to the share of the top 1 and 10 percent. In the un-weighted regressions, the second globalization era seems to have the most significant positive effect and appears to have increased the wealth share of the top 10 percent by 5 percent and the Gini coefficient by 8 percent (though, in this case, only at the 10 percent level). The weighted regressions found that the first period of globalization was positively and significantly associated with an increase in the wealth share of the top 1 percent by 28 percent but the second period of globalization had no significant effects on inequality. As for the post-World War II economic boom era, it appears to have been of little significance in affecting wealth inequality in the un-weighted regression, but in the weighted regression, it is associated with a reduction in the wealth share of the top 1 percent by 9 percent.

In the case of nineteenth century Western frontier land grant policies, there was no significant impact in Canada in mitigating inequality, but in the case of the United States, it does appear to be associated with a decrease in the wealth share of the top 1 and 10 percent at the 10 percent level of significance, at least in the weighted results. The period of Western land settlement policy in the United States, however, does bump up the value of its Gini coefficient by 11 percent, but it is also associated with a 40 percent drop in the wealth share of the top 1 percent and a 9 percent drop in the wealth share of the top 10 percent. Meanwhile, in the un-weighted results, Canadian frontier land policy is associated with a significant 73 percent higher wealth share for the top 1 percent.

Even with land grants to disperse real estate ownership, inequality in nineteenth century Canada was still higher than the late twentieth century. This seems at odds with what can be seen as a Canadian redistributive wealth policy in the late nineteenth and early twentieth century via land grants that actually saw increased inequality despite more dispersed real estate wealth.[29] Indeed, this supports the view of Velasco (2016), who maintains that prairie settlement in Canada was a nation-building project orchestrated by Canadian economic elites who were the main beneficiaries of the project as they alienated land from indigenous peoples and then transferred it from public ownership to private ownership, a substantial portion of which was not to individuals but to corporations. As a result, Canada's economic development may not necessarily have been characterized by more egalitarian land distribution or more 'democratic' processes of social formation.

Unionization rates appear to have been a factor of some importance in reducing wealth inequality. In the un-weighted regressions, the unionization in excess of 25–30 percent of the employment variable significantly reduces the wealth share of the top 10 percent in the United States and the United Kingdom by 8 and 15 percent respectively. It is associated with a reduction of the wealth share of the top 1 percent for the United Kingdom of 21 percent. It also is statistically quite important in reducing wealth inequality in Canada as measured by the Gini coefficient by 9 percent (but only at the 10 percent level). These results are paralleled in the weighted regressions for the United States and the United Kingdom in terms of significance but not for Canada. It suggests that during the twentieth century, higher unionization rates were a factor in shifting wealth away from the top 10 percent and giving rise to somewhat larger middle decile wealth holding classes.

As an additional control, variables were also constructed to control for the data source used to construct the inequality measure in an effort to see if the data source affected inequality. Four variables were specified: Survey data, tax data (either income or estate tax data), probate records, and all other sources (e.g., census, national balance sheets, and land records) with all other sources as the omitted category. In the un-weighted regressions, the results suggest that the data source was not a significant factor in the regression that estimated inequality as measured by the Gini coefficient, though estimates obtained from survey data did have a negative effect but only at the 10 percent level. However, the use of survey and tax data is positively and significantly associated with higher wealth inequality when the wealth share of both the top 1 and 10 percent is estimated. As well, probate data is associated with less inequality with respect to the share of the top 1 percent.[30]

In the weighted results, survey data are negatively and significantly associated with lower wealth inequality when the Gini coefficient is the inequality measure and is positive and significant when the wealth share of the top 1 percent is used. Tax data are positively associated with inequality as measured by both the top 1 and 10 percent wealth shares. Meanwhile, probate records are again associated with less inequality across all of the inequality measures used but most significantly for the top 1 and 10 percent shares. Taken together, these results suggest that all other things given there may be estimates of greater or less inequality, depending on the data sources used.

Homeownership rates greater than two-thirds are a positive and significant factor in raising wealth inequality when the wealth share of the top 1 and 10 percent is considered in the United States and the top 10 percent for Canada. However, for Canada, the relationship is negative and significant (but only at the 10 percent level) when the Gini coefficient is considered. The un-weighted results suggest that when the ownership rates exceed 66 percent, the wealth share of the top 10 percent in the United States is 21 percent greater and the top 1 percent is 35 percent greater. The weighted results for the United States bring it down slightly to only 17 and 32 percent greater, respectively. For Canada, the un-weighted results show that the higher home ownership rate is associated with 29 percent greater wealth share of the top 10 percent but a 13 percent lower Gini coefficient (at the 10 percent level).

It would seem that increased homeownership rates have been a factor driving greater inequality in the United States and to a lesser extent Canada. In the case of the United Kingdom, the home ownership rate greater than 66 percent appears to have had no statistically significant effect on inequality but that is probably the result of the joint effect of the United Kingdom's Housing Act of 1980, which served to raise home ownership rates.

## Notes

1. For a discussion, see Castagnoli and Muliere (1990).
2. For more detailed discussions of inequality measures and their construction, see Cowell (2009).
3. The local polynomial smoothed curves are estimated using STATA 15 and assume the default epanechnikov kernel function (which is said to be the most efficient in minimizing the mean integrated squared error). The bandwidth is also default selected and, in STATA, is chosen by the rule-of-thumb method that provides the asymptotically optimal constant bandwidth by minimizing the conditional weighted mean integrated squared error.

4. Reed (2014) concludes 'the differences between Piketty and Giles are largely due to their treatment of different estimates of the level of wealth inequality in the five different data sources used in the analysis.' https://www.theguardian.com/news/datablog/2014/may/29/piketty-chris-giles-and-wealth-inequality-its-all-about-the-discontinuities
5. See Di Matteo (2017a, b). As another example, Freund and Oliver (2016) provide a data analysis that shows that billionaires in the United States are more dynamic than Europe in that one half of European billionaires inherited their fortunes while only one-third did so in the United States.
6. Author's calculation of real GDP using nominal GDP and the Consumer Price Index from the Jorda-Schularick-Taylor Macro History Data Base.
7. Delong (2003) also notes the sustained increase in inequality brought about in America during the second half of the industrial revolution and, based on estimates of the share of the top 1 percent of wealth held by households (Delong 2003; Figure 3), finds increasing inequality up to 1900 and diminishment afterwards.
8. Boundary effects can disturb non-parametric curve estimates near the two ends of an estimated curve. See Müller (1984).
9. The smoothed results in Appendix 5 suggest the wealth share of the top 10 percent is much higher at over 60 percent, compared to 50 percent in Fig. 5.9.
10. LOWESS is a non-parametric regression technique, which estimates a line of best fit without assuming a specific functional form and is also less sensitive to the presence of data outliers. Fitting a LOWESS curve requires a crucial decision involving the size of the smoothing parameter or bandwidth over which the rolling locally weighted regressions used for estimation process are done. Larger bandwidths provide more smoothing while smaller bandwidths provide more local variation in the final curve. For references on LOWESS, see Cleveland (1979, 1985, 1993).
11. For a discussion of opportunity and abundance, their effect on mobility and status, and the shaping of the American character as people of plenty, see Potter (1954).
12. Of course, the irony in comparing the public components of Canadian and US health spending is that in 2016, while the public share of total health spending in Canada is greater than the United States at 70 percent versus 50 percent, given the much higher amount of health spending overall in the United States, per capita public health spending in US Purchasing Power Parity Dollars is actually higher in the United States at $4606 versus $3249 in Canada. Source: OECD Health Statistics 2017. http://www.oecd.org/els/health-systems/health-data.htm
13. Disney and Luo (2015: 4).
14. Disney and Luo (2015: 2).

15. This is a simple technique for estimating the parameters or coefficients of a regression relationship that minimizes the sum of the squares of the differences between the observed values and the fitted relationship.
16. These are essentially pooled time-series regressions with unbalanced panels and non-continuous time.
17. Taking the log of the dependent variable results in a log-linear specification, which has the advantage that the coefficients can be approximately interpreted as percentages.
18. But only for data points available from western Canada in the data set, namely, Manitoba. The Canadian data for the period prior to 1930 are mainly regional estimates, and the availability of data points for Manitoba allowed for the land policy variable to be more precisely specified.
19. See http://www.thecanadianencyclopedia.ca/en/article/dominion-lands-policy/
20. See http://www.digitalhistory.uh.edu/disp_textbook.cfm?smtID=2&psid=3154
21. See https://ourworldindata.org/war-and-peace/
22. For an overview of globalization, see Williamson (1996a, b).
23. Disney and Luo (2015: 2) note that they believe their paper was the first to attempt a welfare analysis of Right to Buy policies.
24. For the United States, this would be the years 1997–2011. For the United Kingdom, it would be 1988–2007, and for Canada observations after 2001.
25. For example, a distinctive feature of Canada is its low population density and bi-cultural division into English and French. The United Kingdom is a more compact and densely populated country. Canada and the United States share a long border, along which—within 100 kilometers of it—most of the Canadian population resides.
26. For example, Smith and Franklin (1974) use national balance sheet estimates and Internal Revenue Service estate tax data to construct their estimates of the concentration of personal wealth.
27. Given the differences in the relative sizes of the three countries, a weighted OLS regression was also estimated with the weighting variable being the country's population share. The average population for each of these three Anglosphere countries was calculated for the years 1650–1750, 1750–1800, 1800–1850, 1850–1900, 1900–1950, 1950–2000, and the period post-2000. Population shares were estimated by dividing the average population for the period to the sum of the averages of the three countries, and the population share was then assigned to the respective years available in the dataset corresponding to the period. Between 1650 and 2010, the US share of the Anglosphere population rises from 10 to 76 percent, the Canadian share rises from 0 to 8 percent, and the British share falls from 90 to 16 percent. Data sources for the population estimates include the Census of

Canada, Statistics Canada, Eh.Net, and assorted web resources, including http://www.visionofbritain.org.uk/census/SRC_P/6/GB1841ABS_1 and http://www.tacitus.nu/historical-atlas/population/british.htm and https://web.viu.ca/davies/h320/population.colonies.htm

28. Suppose our initial model is specified as $G_i = Z_i'B + v_i$, where $G_i$ is inequality, $Z_i$ is the independent variable, B is the coefficient to be estimated, and $v_i$ is an error term. Defining the inverse of the population share as $M_i$, then the weighted least squares estimator is derived by applying OLS to the transformed model:
$M_i^{1/2} G_i = M_i^{1/2} Z_i'B + v_i$.
29. At the same time, Di Matteo (2012) notes that less inequality was correlated with farm employment and real estate shares of wealth between 1870 and 1930 in Canadian micro data.
30. The negative effect of probate as a source may reflect the fact that probate data generally is biased toward individuals who are older and of higher socioeconomic status, and therefore without consistent estate multiplier or social class adjustments, there might be a tendency for such data to suggest relatively lower inequality relative to other sources.

## References

Castagnoli, E., & Muliere, P. (1990). A Note on Inequality Measures and The Pigou-Dalton Principle of Transfers. In C. Dagum & M. Zenga (Eds.), *Income and Wealth Distribution, Inequality and Poverty*. Berlin: Springer, 1710182.

Cleveland, W. S. (1979). Robust Locally Weighted Regression and Smoothing Scatterplots. *Journal of the American Statistical Association, 74*, 829–836.

Cleveland, W. S. (1985). *The Elements of Graphing*. Monterey: Wadsworth.

Cowell, F. A. (2009, December). Measuring Inequality. http://darp.lse.ac.uk/papersDB/Cowell_measuringinequality3.pdf

Delong, B. (2003). Bequests: An Historical Perspective, Chapter 2. In A. H. Munnell & A. Sundén (Eds.), *Death and Sollars: The Role of Gifts and Bequests in America*. Washington, DC: Brookings Institution Press.

Di Matteo, L. (2012). Land and Inequality in Canada 1870–1930. *Scandinavian Economic History Review, 60*(3), 309–334.

Di Matteo, L. (2016a). Wealth Distribution and the Canadian Middle Class: Historical Evidence and Policy Implications. *Canadian Public Policy, 42*(2), 132–151.

Di Matteo, L. (2017a). Does Egalitarianism Come at a Price? Inequality and Economic Performance in Late Nineteenth Century Ontario. *Social Science History, 41*, 1–30.

Di Matteo, L. (2017b). Major Changes to the Federal Personal Income Tax: 1917–2017. In W. Watson & J. Clemens (Eds.), *Zero to 50 in 100 Years: The*

*History and Development of Canada's Personal Income Tax*. Vancouver: Fraser Institute.

Disney, R., & Luo, G. (2015). *The Right to Buy Public Housing in Britain: A Welfare Analysis* (Working paper W15/05). Institute for Fiscal Studies.

Freund, C., & Oliver, S. (2016). *The Origins of the Superrich: The Billionaire Characteristics Database, Working Paper Series* (Vol. 16-1). Washington, DC: Peterson Institute for International Economics.

Müller, H. G. (1984). Boundary Effects in Nonparametric Curve Estimation Models. In T. Havránek, Z. Šidák, & M. Novák (Eds.), *Compstat 1984*. Heidelberg: Physica.

Piketty, T. (2014). *Capital in the 21st Century*. Cambridge, MA: Harvard University Press.

Potter, D. M. (1954). *People of Plenty: Economic Abundance and the American Character*. Chicago: University of Chicago Press.

Reed, H. (2014, May 29). Piketty, Chris Giles and Wealth Inequality: It's All About the Discontinuities. *The Guardian*. https://www.theguardian.com/news/datablog/2014/may/29/piketty-chris-giles-and-wealth-inequality-its-all-about-the-discontinuities

Reeves, R. V. (2017). *Dream Hoarders. How the American Upper Middle Class Is Leaving Everyone Else in the Dust*. Washington, DC: Brooking.

Roine, J., & Waldenström, D. (2015). Long-Run Trends in the Distribution of Income and Wealth. In A. B. Atkinson & F. Bourguignon (Eds.), *Handbook of Income Distribution* (Vol. 2A). Amsterdam: Elsevier.

Smith, J. C., & Franklin, S. D. (1974). The Concentration of Personal Wealth, 1922–1969. *American Economic Review: Papers and Proceedings, 64*(2), 162–167.

Sutch, R. (2017). The One Percent Across Two Centuries: A Replication of Thomas Piketty's Data on the Concentration of Wealth in the United States. *Social Science History, 41*(4), 587–613.

Velasco, G. F. (2016). *Natural Resources, State Formation and the Institutions of Settler Capitalism: The Case of Western Canada, 1850–1914*. PhD Thesis, London School of Economics and Political Science.

Williamson, J. G. (1996a). *Globalization and Inequality Then and Now: The Late 19th and Late 20th Centuries Compared*. National Bureau of Economic Research, Working Paper 5491.

Williamson, J. G. (1996b). Globalization, Convergence and History. *The Journal of Economic History, 56*(2), 277–306.

CHAPTER 6

# Summary and Concluding Thoughts: The Persistence of Wealth Inequality

**Abstract** Wealth inequality is driven by complex interacting forces and the outcome of economic change. The long-term trend in wealth inequality is for it to be pushed up by the forces of economic growth and industrialization in line with a Kuznets curve type story, but mitigating factors can pull it back down as during the twentieth century. Along with increased unionization rates, there were government policy factors such as estate taxation and the fostering of home ownership. A reduction in union strength as well as the end of estate taxation and less progressive income tax systems may be factors raising economic inequality since the 1970s, especially when combined with lower economic growth rates in relation to rates of return to capital as like with Piketty's story.

**Keywords** Inequality • Economic change • Mitigation

This study has conducted an examination of wealth inequality focusing on the North Atlantic Anglosphere countries of the United Kingdom, Canada, and the United States over the period stretching from approximately 1668 to 2013. The wealth inequality data examined are a compilation of assorted estimates for Gini coefficients and the wealth shares of the top 1 and 10 percent of the wealth distribution. This longer-term perspective affords an



L. Di Matteo, *The Evolution and Determinants of Wealth Inequality in the North Atlantic Anglo-Sphere, 1668–2013*,
https://doi.org/10.1007/978-3-319-89773-8_6

opportunity to examine whether the era of industrialization was associated with rising or falling wealth inequality as well as what the trends have been during the twentieth century. A key advantage of using these three countries is that they share many common features with respect to history, language, institutions, economy, trade, and culture given the historical settlement and colonial relationship between Canada and the United States with respect to Great Britain. Moreover, there remain substantial current economic and political links.

Prior to 1750, wealth inequality was higher in the United Kingdom than in the United States, but inequality grew rapidly in the United States to the point where it matched the United Kingdom's inequality by the mid-nineteenth century. The preindustrial period does appear to have been marked by lower wealth inequality not only in the United States but also in the United Kingdom. The subsequent era of industrialization does appear to have been marked in all three Anglosphere countries by rising wealth inequality. As inequality does appear to have been lower in both the United Kingdom and the United States prior to industrialization, this suggests that the more agriculturally intensive stage of economic development was associated with lower wealth inequality.

The evidence for Canada, the United States, and the United Kingdom also shows reduced wealth inequality starting in the twentieth century after the increases of industrialization. However, despite the mitigation, the level of inequality remains high in all three countries as captured by the three measures used here—Gini coefficients and the wealth shares of the top 1 and 10 percent. Indeed, wealth inequality has been high and persistent throughout the period of this study, though some eras have seen lower wealth inequality than others. Indeed, wealth inequality has generally been higher than income inequality despite the preoccupation with the latter.

While the twentieth century saw the inequality of wealth decline and a wealth transfer away from the top 1 and 10 percent of the distribution, the period since the 1970s sees a small increase in wealth inequality in Canada but a much larger increase in the United States. However, the United Kingdom while still marked by high wealth inequality—indeed the top 10 percent still own approximately 50 percent of the wealth—it nevertheless is not marked by a rebound like that of the United States. Indeed, the United Kingdom's trend in wealth inequality more closely resembles some of the European countries, including the Nordic ones.

By the early twenty-first century, both Canada and the United Kingdom see their top 10 percent owning approximately 50 percent of the wealth and the United States over 70 percent. Meanwhile, the top 1 percent own just under 20 percent in Canada and the United Kingdom, while in the United states, the share is closer to 35 percent.

When these trends are examined within the additional context of regression analysis to ascertain the long-term determinants and correlates of wealth inequality, the results suggest that there are several narratives with regards to the evolution of wealth inequality that are at once both similar and different. In all three countries, the long-term trend in wealth inequality is for it to be pushed up by the forces of economic growth and industrialization, much along the lines of a Kuznets Curve type story. However, there are mitigating factors that then serve to pull it back down, especially during the twentieth century.

Periods of economic globalization appear to have had some impact on raising wealth inequality, especially as measured by the wealth shares of the top 1 and 10 percent. Furthermore, these trends are also consistent with Piketty's thesis given that interest rates have generally exceeded growth rates of the economy most of the time—the post-war boom period from 1945 to 1973 being a key exception. Yet it is not an inexorable upward trend, and countervailing forces and pressures have emerged in all three countries, which have operated to reduce inequality. The post-war boom period in particular appears to have had some effect in especially reducing the wealth shares of the top 1 percent.

From the middle of the seventeenth century and into the late nineteenth century, wealth inequality had a tendency to rise. However, from the late nineteenth and into the mid-twentieth century, there was a mitigation of wealth inequality in all three countries. This mitigation is strongly correlated with a number of factors that appear to have pulled inequality downward. Given that most of these countries had industrialized by the mid-twentieth century, a fall in inequality certainly supports a Kuznets story of inequality falling after the rapid growth of industrialization. These patterns also supports Piketty's dynamic given that rates of return to capital were generally higher than the rate of growth of the economy, particularly prior to World War II and as economies slowed and interest rates rose after the oil price shocks of the 1970s.

The factors operating to pull down inequality also reflect institutional and policy factors that had more important effects in the first half of the twentieth century and then weakened, allowing wealth inequality to rebound upward—particularly in the United States. Along with factors such as increased unionization rates, rising public spending on health and education and larger public sectors, and increased home ownership (especially for the United Kingdom), there were explicit government policy factors such as estate taxation, more progressive income tax systems, and in the case of the United Kingdom, the housing policy that resulted in the disposition and dispersion of much public housing into private hands. A reduction in the strength of unions as measured by unionization rates as well as the end of estate taxation and the implementation of less progressive income tax systems may all be factors serving to raise economic inequality since the 1970s, especially when combined with lower economic growth rates in relation to rates of return to capital.

It also remains that in the end, Canadian wealth inequality has remained below that of the United States and the United Kingdom for most of the time period under consideration and has grown closer to that of the United Kingdom more recently. Despite some recent increases in wealth inequality, relative to the United States and the United Kingdom, Canada has not been characterized by as large a set of shifts in wealth distribution over time. At the same time, some of the myths that characterize Canadian views of wealth distribution—such as the assumed leveling effect of prairie land settlement policies—at least statistically do not seem to be supported by the evidence. The view of Canada as a more egalitarian society relative to the extremes of both the United States and the United Kingdom is also not always supported by the evidence. After controlling for other factors, the wealth share of the top 1 percent in Canada is not always significantly lower than that of those other two countries.

Yet, one key difference between Canada relative to the United States and the United Kingdom has been Canada's continued greater relative reliance on natural resources as an economic driver, but how such a correlation with lower wealth inequality might actually operate to reduce inequality is unclear. While natural resource activities in forestry and mining were historically labor intensive—perhaps serving to generate high and dispersed amounts of labor income and ultimately wealth—given that these sectors have become less labor intensive over time, this should be expected to correlate with a surge in inequality. Such a surge is not detected given the evidence here using the wealth shares of the top 10 percent or Gini coefficients. It may be any such effects have been counterbalanced by relatively more stable rates of unionization in Canada.

Unlike the United States, which has seen resurgence in the wealth and income shares of the top decile over the last few decades, there has not been as noticeably large a rebound in the wealth inequality in Canada with the exception of the top 1 percent, though even this is nowhere near what has happened in the United States. This is all the more remarkable given the increasing economic integration of Canada and the United States since the advent of the Free Trade Agreement (1988) and the North American Free Trade Agreement (NAFTA) (1994), which one might expect to be somewhat of a force for convergence in inequality patterns given the potential for economic standardization in matters such as wages and labor laws, as well as regulatory policy in general.[1]

In the Canadian case, these regression results also raise the question as to why wealth inequality has not been as correlated with rising income inequality, especially given the rise in Canadian housing prices and rates of homeownership since the early 1990s, which one might expect to affect wealth distribution. It is worth noting that for the United States, over the period of the late twentieth and early twenty-first centuries, income inequality increased more than wealth inequality, until the period of the Great Recession—when wealth inequality especially surged. Wolff (2016) explains the increase in wealth inequality after 2009 as the result of huge negative return on net worth of middle wealth deciles, which dropped median net worth between 2007 and 2010 that, in turn, was due to the drop in highly leveraged housing prices. This explains perhaps why higher rates of homeownership in the United States have also been correlated with high wealth inequality.

It is also noteworthy that high rates of home ownership were associated with greater wealth inequality—more so in the United States but less so in Canada and the United Kingdom. This suggests that the collapse of housing prices can be a factor in affecting wealth distribution, and unlike the United States, housing prices in the wake of the 2008–2009 Great Recession were not as adversely affected in the United Kingdom or Canada. In the Canadian case, despite high and increasing household debt levels which now resemble those of the United States prior to 2009, there has yet to be a steep drop in real estate prices that might yield effects similar to the United States with respect to their effect on wealth inequality, given the tendency of the middle class to emphasize real estate in their wealth portfolios.

The effectiveness of factors and forces serving to mitigate wealth inequality vary across these three countries. The higher estate tax regimes of the twentieth century are correlated with reductions in wealth inequality but appear to have been most effective in the United Kingdom. As a result, the recent changes in both the United States and the United Kingdom toward higher exemptions in their current estate tax regimes can be expected to play a part in either maintaining or increasing current levels of wealth inequality.

Unionization rates have also been a factor in reducing the wealth share of the top 10 percent in the United States and the United Kingdom but less so in Canada where unionization's effect on reducing inequality is more evident with respect to the Gini coefficient. As for higher rates of home ownership, they seem to have been a factor of some consequence in reducing wealth inequality in Canada and the United Kingdom but not so in the United States. Again, for the United States, these effects appear to be more significant in affecting the top 1 and 10 percent wealth shares.

In the end, wealth inequality is driven by complex interacting forces and not necessarily by simple inexorable laws relating rates of return and accumulation. Moreover, changes in wealth inequality are also the outcome of the process of economic change. Economic change via war, globalization, technological change, and booms can manage to create both winners and losers, and it is the balance between these winners and losers that drives changes in inequality. For economic change to occur, it inevitably must cause some individuals to forge ahead in their wealth accumulation as they take advantage of new opportunities giving rise to more wealth dispersion and inequality. If one wants changes in wealth distribution to stop, then it can be ventured that one must also be prepared to limit economic change from forces such as technological progress and innovation.

Wealth inequality in the North Atlantic Anglosphere has been shaped by similar forces but with a variation across these three countries as a result of differential impacts of these forces. The impact of industrialization, globalization, and associated economic change has been to raise wealth inequality, but there have been policy and institutional responses that have then served to mitigate the effects. If one thinks of wealth inequality as a batch of bread dough with a natural tendency to rise, then from time to time there have been forces and factors that have served to punch the bread dough back down. What should be of greater concern is not the short-term effects of economic change on wealth inequality per se but if the wealth inequality arising from economic change becomes fossilized and permanently entrenched. This is indeed the greater long-term policy problem and represents the challenge to not only to the North Atlantic Anglosphere but indeed all countries.

## Note

1. It should be noted that Canada and the United States have shared common regulatory policies in the past that predate NAFTA, such as the 1909 Boundary Waters Treaty as well as acid rain agreements, not to mention the Canada-US Automobile Pact of the 1960s.

## Reference

Wolff, E. N. (2016). Household Wealth Trends in the United States, 1962 to 2013: What Happened over the Great Recession? *Russell Sage Foundation Journal of the Social Sciences, 2*(6), 24–43.

# Appendices

## Appendix 1

### *Data Tables Used for Construction of Canadian Wealth Inequality Estimates Using Federal Succession Duty and Estate Tax Data: 1950–1952 and 1959–1960*

**Estate income 1950**

| *Income class* | *Number* | *Income per estate ($)* |
|---|---|---|
| LT $1000 | 2660 | 188 |
| $1000–1500 | 190 | 1100 |
| 1500–2000 | 170 | 1729 |
| 2000–2500 | 140 | 2186 |
| 2500–3000 | 130 | 2777 |
| 3000–3500 | 100 | 3240 |
| 3500–4000 | 70 | 3771 |
| 4000–4500 | 40 | 4225 |
| 4500–5000 | 50 | 4620 |
| 5000–6000 | 70 | 5586 |
| 6000–7000 | 30 | 6700 |
| 7000–8000 | 30 | 7200 |
| 8000–9000 | 30 | 8200 |

(*continued*)



L. Di Matteo, *The Evolution and Determinants of Wealth Inequality in the North Atlantic Anglo-Sphere, 1668–2013*,
https://doi.org/10.1007/978-3-319-89773-8

(continued)

| *Income class* | *Number* | *Income per estate ($)* |
|---|---|---|
| 9000–10,000 | 30 | 9667 |
| 10,000–15,000 | 100 | 11,930 |
| Over 15,000 | 150 | 37,713 |
| **Total** | **3990** | |

Source: Estates (Table J, p.119) Department of National Revenue, Taxation Division, Taxation Statistics 1952, Queen's Printer, Ottawa, Canada

## Estate income 1951

| *Income class* | *Number* | *Income per estate ($)* |
|---|---|---|
| LT $1000 | 2640 | 203 |
| $1000–1500 | 230 | 1230 |
| 1500–2000 | 250 | 1756 |
| 2000–2500 | 340 | 2229 |
| 2500–3000 | 230 | 2717 |
| 3000–3500 | 200 | 3235 |
| 3500–4000 | 80 | 3775 |
| 4000–4500 | 90 | 4267 |
| 4500–5000 | 70 | 4743 |
| 5000–6000 | 90 | 5511 |
| 6000–7000 | 70 | 6629 |
| 7000–8000 | 70 | 7443 |
| 8000–9000 | 60 | 8500 |
| 9000–10,000 | 20 | 9500 |
| 10,000–15,000 | 100 | 11,420 |
| Over 15,000 | 70 | 34,743 |
| **Total** | **4610** | |

Source: Estates (Table 10, p. 71), Department of National Revenue, Taxation Division, Taxation Statistics 1953, Queen's Printer, Ottawa, Canada

## Estate income 1952

| *Income class* | *Number* | *Income per estate ($)* |
|---|---|---|
| LT $1000 | 1520 | 371 |
| $1000–1500 | 650 | 1326 |
| 1500–2000 | 440 | 1930 |
| 2000–2500 | 390 | 2274 |
| 2500–3000 | 340 | 2738 |
| 3000–3500 | 310 | 3113 |
| 3500–4000 | 280 | 3754 |

(*continued*)

(continued)

| *Income class* | *Number* | *Income per estate ($)* |
|---|---|---|
| 4000–4500 | 160 | 4213 |
| 4500–5000 | 120 | 4783 |
| 5000–6000 | 210 | 5452 |
| 6000–7000 | 200 | 6330 |
| 7000–8000 | 120 | 7367 |
| 8000–9000 | 100 | 8550 |
| 9000–10,000 | 0 | 0 |
| 10,000–15,000 | 350 | 12,091 |
| Over 15,000 | 310 | 41,152 |
| **Total** | **5500** | |

Source: Estates (Table 10, p. 70), Department of National Revenue, Taxation Division, Taxation Statistics 1954, Queen's Printer, Ottawa, Canada

## Taxable Canadian domiciled estates by size of estate, fiscal year 1959–1960

| *Size of estate ($)* | *Number* | *Net value per estate ($)* |
|---|---|---|
| ***0–24,999***[a] | **1197** | **12,500** |
| ***25,000–49,999*** | **818** | **37,500** |
| 50,000–74,999 | 763 | 62,872 |
| 75,000–99,999 | 481 | 86,667 |
| 100,000–124,999 | 262 | 110,870 |
| 125,000–149,999 | 146 | 135,815 |
| 150,000–199,999 | 166 | 172,169 |
| 200,000–299,999 | 113 | 247,097 |
| 300,000–399,999 | 59 | 341,949 |
| 400,000–499,999 | 26 | 437,423 |
| 500,000–599,999 | 12 | 553,417 |
| 600,000–699,999 | 12 | 639,667 |
| 700,000–799,999 | 6 | 729,667 |
| 800,000–899,999 | 8 | 852,750 |
| 900,000–999,999 | 5 | 943,400 |
| 1,000,000 and over | 18 | 1,586,222 |
| Total | **4092** | |

[a]Number estimated via exponential interpolation

$y = 1751.7e^{-0381x}$

R-sq = 0.88738

Source: Table 2, Estate Tax

Department of National Revenue, Taxation Division, Taxation Statistics 1961, Queen's Printer, Ottawa, Canada

**Taxable Canadian domiciled estates by size of estate, fiscal year 1960–1961**

| *Size of estate ($)* | *Number* | *Net value per estate ($)* |
|---|---|---|
| **0–24,999**[a] | **2189** | **12,500** |
| **25,000–49,999** | **1487** | **37,500** |
| 50,000–74999 | 1142 | 62988 |
| 75,000–99999 | 781 | 86347 |
| 100,000–124,999 | 403 | 111,256 |
| 125,000–149,999 | 301 | 136,784 |
| 150,000–199,999 | 287 | 171,986 |
| 200,000–299,999 | 256 | 242,859 |
| 300,000–399,999 | 116 | 344,284 |
| 400,000–499,999 | 53 | 449,736 |
| 500,000–599,999 | 27 | 547,667 |
| 600,000–699,999 | 23 | 645,087 |
| 700,000–799,999 | 11 | 747,455 |
| 800,000–899,999 | 4 | 829,750 |
| 900,000–999,999 | 11 | 952,091 |
| 1,000,000 and over | 37 | 1,873,973 |
| **Total** | **7128** | |

[a]Number estimated via exponential interpolation
$y = 3223.5e^{-0387x}$
R-sq = 0.85191

Source: Table 2, Estate Tax
Department of National Revenue, Taxation Division, Taxation Statistics 1962, Queen's Printer, Ottawa, Canada

# Appendix 2

## *Estimates of Wealth Inequality for Canada, 1851–2012*

| | *Year* | *Gini* | *Top 1 percent* | *Top 10 percent* |
|---|---|---|---|---|
| Thunder Bay District[a] | 1887 | 0.718 | 14.6 | 64.9 |
| | 1892 | 0.647 | 5.8 | 47.8 |
| | 1897 | 0.646 | 9.1 | 49.7 |
| | 1902 | 0.771 | 18.5 | 69.3 |
| | 1907 | 0.740 | 13.0 | 66.5 |
| | 1912 | 0.776 | 18.6 | 65.0 |
| | 1917 | 0.732 | 18.7 | 64.0 |
| | 1922 | 0.666 | 10.8 | 56.5 |
| | 1927 | 0.833 | 19.0 | 81.0 |
| Ontario[a] | 1892 | 0.687 | 26.1 | 58.3 |
| | 1902 | 0.670 | 23.2 | 55.1 |

(*continued*)

(continued)

| | Year | Gini | Top 1 percent | Top 10 percent |
|---|---|---|---|---|
| Toronto[b] | 1861 | 0.656 | | 53.9 |
| | 1871 | 0.690 | | 56.2 |
| | 1881 | 0.661 | | 56.1 |
| | 1891 | 0.624 | | 49.4 |
| | 1899 | 0.598 | | 49.9 |
| Manitoba[c] | 1875 | 0.695 | 7.9 | 53.8 |
| | 1882 | 0.656 | 7.8 | 48.7 |
| | 1887 | 0.831 | 15.2 | 73.5 |
| | 1892 | 0.643 | 7.3 | 49.6 |
| | 1897 | 0.690 | 16.1 | 55.3 |
| | 1902 | 0.716 | 25.7 | 61.9 |
| | 1907 | 0.689 | 23.3 | 56.3 |
| | 1912 | 0.905 | 45.7 | 88.1 |
| | 1917 | 0.664 | 8.6 | 46.4 |
| | 1922 | 0.747 | 26.6 | 62.2 |
| | 1927 | 0.642 | 11.0 | 44.1 |
| Canada[d] | 1970 | 0.716 | | 53.3 |
| | 1977 | 0.742 | 27.0 | 60.3 |
| | 1984 | 0.686 | 16.7 | 51.9 |
| | 1999 | 0.727 | 16.2 | 51.5 |
| | 2005 | 0.741 | 20.1 | 60.1 |
| | 2012 | 0.648 | 12.8 | 47.2 |
| Nova Scotia[e] | 1851 | 0.620 | | 53.9 |
| | 1871 | 0.740 | | 68.5 |
| Wentworth County[f] | 1872 | 0.686 | 8.7 | 57.8 |
| | 1882 | 0.620 | 9.4 | 48.5 |
| | 1892 | 0.734 | 16.1 | 58.1 |
| | 1902 | 0.739 | 22.1 | 62.3 |
| | 1907 | 0.747 | 26.1 | 64.0 |
| | 1912 | 0.718 | 24.7 | 61.4 |
| | 1917 | 0.771 | 30.3 | 69.5 |
| | 1922 | 0.709 | 20.9 | 58.4 |
| | 1927 | 0.734 | 29.5 | 63.9 |
| Canada[g] | 1950 | 0.810 | 13.9 | 73.4 |
| | 1951 | 0.711 | 15.9 | 56.0 |
| | 1952 | 0.662 | 7.9 | 55.0 |
| Canada[h] | 1959 | 0.551 | 14.2 | 43.7 |
| | 1960 | 0.584 | 17.3 | 46.7 |
| Canada[i] | 2000 | 0.688 | | 53.0 |

(*continued*)

(continued)

Notes
[a]1887–1902 done for five years—two years before and after due to smaller sample size. For example, 1885–1889; 1907 done for three years, for example, 1906–1908. For details on the Ontario, Wentworth County, Manitoba, and Thunder Bay data sets, see Di Matteo (2004, 2012, 2013a, 2016a, b)
[b]Real estate only taken from assessment rolls. See Darroch (1983) Early Industrialization and Inequality in Toronto, 1861–1899 Labour/Le Travailleur, 11 (Spring), 31–61
[c]Done for years before and after—due to smaller sample size. For example, 1873–1877 for 1875, 1881 to 1883 for 1882; three years afterward 1886–1888 for 1887, 1891–1893 for 1892, and so on
[d]1970 and 1977 from Oja (1987). Changes in the Distribution of Wealth in Canada, 1970–1984. Statistics Canada 13-588-no 1.; 1984, 2005, and 2012 calculated from SCF & SFS public use microdata files. The 1999 values from Morisette et al. (2002). Networth valued on termination basis
[e]From Gwyn and Siddiq (1992)
[f]Wentworth County 1872–1902 Di Matteo and George (1992) Table 3
[g]Canada. Calculated from Estate Income Data. Taxation Statistics. Department of Revenue. Based on income from estates
[h]Canada. Calculated from Estate Tax Data. Taxation Statistics. Department of Revenue. Based on net estate value and adjusted with interpolation for estate numbers below $50,000
[i]Davies et al. (2011) Table 7, p. 246

# Appendix 3

## *Estimates of Wealth Inequality for the United States, 1680–2012*

| | *Year* | *Gini* | *Top 1 percent* | *Top 10 percent* |
|---|---|---|---|---|
| United States[a] | 1774 | | | 59.0 |
| | 1890 | | | 72.2 |
| | 1962 | | | 64.6 |
| | 1983 | | | 68.9 |
| | 1989 | | | 67.2 |
| | 1992 | | | 67.1 |
| | 1995 | | | 67.8 |
| | 1998 | | | 68.6 |
| | 2001 | | | 69.8 |
| | 2004 | | | 69.5 |
| | 2007 | | | 71.5 |
| | 2010 | | | 74.5 |
| United States[b] | 1720 | 0.590 | | |
| | 1730 | 0.630 | | |
| | 1740 | 0.610 | | |
| | 1750 | 0.610 | | |
| | 1760 | 0.660 | | |
| | 1785 | 0.710 | | |
| | 1790 | 0.710 | | |
| | 1795 | 0.710 | | |

(*continued*)

(continued)

| | Year | Gini | Top 1 percent | Top 10 percent |
|---|---|---|---|---|
| | 1800 | 0.680 | | |
| | 1805 | 0.660 | | |
| | 1680 | 0.510 | | |
| | 1690 | 0.600 | | |
| | 1700 | 0.570 | | |
| | 1710 | 0.600 | | |
| | 1720 | 0.570 | | |
| | 1730 | 0.560 | | |
| | 1740 | 0.540 | | |
| | 1750 | 0.540 | | |
| | 1769 | 0.590 | | |
| | 1770 | 0.590 | | |
| | 1790 | 0.620 | | |
| | 1800 | 0.640 | | |
| | 1688 | 0.530 | | |
| | 1746 | 0.680 | | |
| | 1767 | 0.650 | | |
| | 1796 | 0.810 | | |
| | 1829 | 0.860 | | |
| | 1859 | 0.850 | | |
| | 1774 | 0.730 | | 58 |
| | 1798 | 0.750 | | 55 |
| | 1771 | 0.789 | | |
| | 1798 | 0.820 | | |
| | 1798 | 0.780 | | |
| | 1860 | 0.832 | | |
| | 1983 | 0.802 | | |
| United States[c] | 1910 | | 45.10 | 81.13 |
| | 1920 | | 43.70 | 79.73 |
| | 1930 | | 37.40 | 73.41 |
| | 1940 | | 30.40 | 66.39 |
| | 1950 | | 29.70 | 65.67 |
| | 1960 | | 31.40 | 67.00 |
| | 1970 | | 28.20 | 64.18 |
| | 1980 | | 30.10 | 67.20 |
| | 1990 | | 32.90 | 68.70 |
| | 2000 | | 33.10 | 69.65 |
| | 2010 | | 33.80 | 71.50 |
| | 1810 | | 25.00 | 58.00 |
| | 1870 | | 32.00 | 71.00 |
| United States[d] | 1962 | 0.76 | | 62.00 |
| | 1973 | 0.81 | | 69.80 |
| | 1916 | | 38.12 | |

*(continued)*

(continued)

| | *Year* | *Gini* | *Top 1 percent* | *Top 10 percent* |
|---|---|---|---|---|
| United States[e] | 1917 | | 35.58 | |
| | 1918 | | 36.80 | |
| | 1919 | | 39.93 | |
| | 1920 | | 37.61 | |
| | 1921 | | 35.22 | |
| | 1922 | | 36.02 | |
| | 1923 | | 35.22 | |
| | 1924 | | 36.70 | |
| | 1925 | | 36.02 | |
| | 1926 | | 35.15 | |
| | 1927 | | 39.21 | |
| | 1928 | | 36.50 | |
| | 1929 | | 36.76 | |
| | 1930 | | 40.29 | |
| | 1931 | | 34.70 | |
| | 1932 | | 28.40 | |
| | 1933 | | 30.31 | |
| | 1934 | | 28.09 | |
| | 1935 | | 27.77 | |
| | 1936 | | 29.70 | |
| | 1937 | | 26.97 | |
| | 1938 | | 27.06 | |
| | 1939 | | 25.95 | |
| | 1940 | | 25.27 | |
| | 1941 | | 25.30 | |
| | 1942 | | 23.74 | |
| | 1943 | | 24.26 | |
| | 1944 | | 25.49 | |
| | 1945 | | 24.65 | |
| | 1946 | | 24.49 | |
| | 1947 | | 24.28 | |
| | 1948 | | 23.04 | |
| | 1949 | | 22.59 | |
| | 1950 | | 22.78 | |
| | 1953 | | 23.77 | |
| | 1954 | | 23.18 | |
| | 1956 | | 24.75 | |
| | 1958 | | 24.18 | |
| | 1960 | | 25.25 | |
| | 1962 | | 24.39 | |
| | 1965 | | 24.70 | |
| | 1969 | | 22.86 | |
| | 1972 | | 23.13 | |
| | 1976 | | 19.32 | |

(*continued*)

(continued)

| | *Year* | *Gini* | *Top 1 percent* | *Top 10 percent* |
|---|---|---|---|---|
| | 1982 | | 19.06 | |
| | 1983 | | 21.07 | |
| | 1984 | | 20.95 | |
| | 1985 | | 22.35 | |
| | 1986 | | 22.66 | |
| | 1987 | | 21.57 | |
| | 1988 | | 21.70 | |
| | 1989 | | 21.96 | |
| | 1990 | | 20.86 | |
| | 1991 | | 21.54 | |
| | 1992 | | 21.18 | |
| | 1993 | | 21.31 | |
| | 1994 | | 21.58 | |
| | 1995 | | 21.54 | |
| | 1996 | | 21.45 | |
| | 1997 | | 21.24 | |
| | 1998 | | 21.70 | |
| | 1999 | | 21.68 | |
| | 2000 | | 20.79 | |
| United States[f] | 1774 | 0.730 | 14.60 | 54.8 |
| | 1774 | 0.800 | 20.90 | 56.8 |
| | 1774 | 0.600 | 13.70 | 42.1 |
| | 1774 | 0.680 | 11.30 | 48.8 |
| | 1860 | 0.830 | | 73.0 |
| | 1870 | 0.810 | | 68.0 |
| | 1870 | 0.830 | | 70.0 |
| | 1962 | 0.760 | | 62.0 |
| | 1890 | | | 72.0 |
| | 1848 | 0.860 | 37.00 | |
| | 1841 | 0.870 | 42.00 | |
| | 1922 | | 32.00 | |
| | 1929 | | 36.00 | |
| | 1933 | | 28.00 | |
| | 1939 | | 31.00 | |
| | 1945 | | 23.00 | |
| | 1949 | | 21.00 | |
| | 1953 | | 24.00 | |
| | 1956 | | 26.00 | |
| | 1958 | | 27.00 | |
| | 1962 | | 27.00 | |
| | 1965 | | 29.00 | |
| | 1969 | | 25.00 | |
| | 1972 | | 27.00 | |
| | 1962 | 0.760 | 34.00 | 62.0 |

*(continued)*

(continued)

| | *Year* | *Gini* | *Top 1 percent* | *Top 10 percent* |
|---|---|---|---|---|
| United States[g] | 1774 | 0.694 | | 53.2 |
| | 1860 | 0.832 | | 73.0 |
| | 1870 | 0.833 | | 70.0 |
| | 1962 | 0.720 | | |
| | 1969 | 0.720 | | |
| | 1983 | 0.720 | | |
| | 1986 | 0.720 | | |
| United States[h] | 1984 | 0.807 | | |
| | 1989 | 0.798 | | |
| | 1994 | 0.796 | | |
| | 1999 | 0.818 | | |
| | 2001 | 0.813 | | |
| | 2003 | 0.814 | | |
| | 2005 | 0.815 | | |
| | 2007 | 0.832 | | |
| | 2009 | 0.890 | | |
| | 2011 | 0.879 | | |
| United States[i] | 2000 | 0.801 | | |
| United States[j] | 1810 | | | 69.0 |
| | 1860 | | | 71.0 |
| | 1860 | | | 72.0 |
| | 1900 | | | 73.0 |
| | 1900 | | | 74.0 |
| United States[k] | 1913 | | 44.0 | |
| | 1914 | | 44.1 | |
| | 1915 | | 43.8 | |
| | 1916 | | 42.7 | |
| | 1917 | | 41.1 | 79.5 |
| | 1918 | | 37.4 | 77.8 |
| | 1919 | | 40.0 | 79.4 |
| | 1920 | | 35.6 | 77.3 |
| | 1921 | | 35.9 | 77.4 |
| | 1922 | | 39.1 | 78.6 |
| | 1923 | | 34.7 | 79.3 |
| | 1924 | | 36.8 | 80.7 |
| | 1925 | | 43.1 | 82.3 |
| | 1926 | | 45.1 | 83.0 |
| | 1927 | | 49.5 | 83.9 |
| | 1928 | | 51.4 | 84.4 |
| | 1929 | | 50.6 | 84.3 |
| | 1930 | | 49.0 | 83.6 |
| | 1931 | | 48.0 | 83.6 |

*(continued)*

(continued)

| *Year* | *Gini* | *Top 1 percent* | *Top 10 percent* |
|---|---|---|---|
| 1932 | | 47.0 | 84.0 |
| 1933 | | 47.1 | 84.1 |
| 1934 | | 47.2 | 82.5 |
| 1935 | | 45.3 | 81.2 |
| 1936 | | 45.2 | 81.6 |
| 1937 | | 45.3 | 79.9 |
| 1938 | | 40.7 | 79.7 |
| 1939 | | 41.9 | 80.1 |
| 1940 | | 37.9 | 77.6 |
| 1941 | | 35.0 | 76.2 |
| 1942 | | 34.6 | 74.7 |
| 1943 | | 35.1 | 75.2 |
| 1944 | | 34.5 | 74.9 |
| 1945 | | 34.4 | 75.2 |
| 1946 | | 31.8 | 74.6 |
| 1947 | | 30.2 | 73.0 |
| 1948 | | 29.9 | 71.9 |
| 1949 | | 29.1 | 71.1 |
| 1950 | | 30.5 | 71.6 |
| 1951 | | 30.0 | 71.4 |
| 1952 | | 29.7 | 71.1 |
| 1953 | | 28.3 | 70.3 |
| 1954 | | 28.8 | 70.6 |
| 1955 | | 29.1 | 71.0 |
| 1956 | | 29.4 | 71.3 |
| 1957 | | 29.2 | 71.8 |
| 1958 | | 28.9 | 71.8 |
| 1959 | | 29.4 | 72.5 |
| 1960 | | 29.4 | 72.7 |
| 1961 | | 29.4 | 72.9 |
| 1962 | | 29.6 | 73.6 |
| 1963 | | 29.1 | 73.1 |
| 1964 | | 28.5 | 72.7 |
| 1965 | | 28.4 | 72.2 |
| 1966 | | 28.3 | 71.7 |
| 1967 | | 27.8 | 70.8 |
| 1968 | | 28.6 | 70.5 |
| 1969 | | 27.9 | 70.1 |
| 1970 | | 27.6 | 70.0 |
| 1971 | | 27.0 | 69.9 |
| 1972 | | 26.5 | 69.7 |
| 1973 | | 24.9 | 69.1 |
| 1974 | | 24.9 | 68.5 |

(*continued*)

(continued)

| *Year* | *Gini* | *Top 1 percent* | *Top 10 percent* |
|---|---|---|---|
| 1975 | | 24.7 | 68.2 |
| 1976 | | 23.5 | 67.7 |
| 1977 | | 23.9 | 67.2 |
| 1978 | | 22.9 | 66.8 |
| 1979 | | 24.4 | 67.4 |
| 1980 | | 24.3 | 67.1 |
| 1981 | | 25.3 | 67.0 |
| 1982 | | 25.7 | 65.9 |
| 1983 | | 24.7 | 65.0 |
| 1984 | | 24.8 | 64.4 |
| 1985 | | 25.1 | 63.7 |
| 1986 | | 25.1 | 63.6 |
| 1987 | | 26.2 | 64.3 |
| 1988 | | 27.9 | 65.3 |
| 1989 | | 27.8 | 65.2 |
| 1990 | | 28.1 | 65.7 |
| 1991 | | 27.6 | 65.5 |
| 1992 | | 29.2 | 67.1 |
| 1993 | | 29.5 | 67.5 |
| 1994 | | 29.2 | 67.4 |
| 1995 | | 29.5 | 67.6 |
| 1996 | | 30.3 | 68.0 |
| 1997 | | 31.2 | 68.6 |
| 1998 | | 32.3 | 69.2 |
| 1999 | | 33.3 | 69.5 |
| 2000 | | 34.1 | 69.8 |
| 2001 | | 33.2 | 69.2 |
| 2002 | | 32.0 | 69.0 |
| 2003 | | 32.3 | 69.3 |
| 2004 | | 33.5 | 70.0 |
| 2005 | | 34.0 | 69.9 |
| 2006 | | 34.9 | 70.7 |
| 2007 | | 36.0 | 71.6 |
| 2008 | | 38.1 | 74.6 |
| 2009 | | 37.8 | 75.1 |
| 2010 | | 39.5 | 75.7 |
| 2011 | | 39.8 | 76.0 |
| 2012 | | 41.8 | 77.2 |

Notes

[a]Source: Roine and Waldenstrom (2014) Tables A1–A4, Roine and Waldenstrom (2014) Long-Run Trends in the Distribution of Income and Wealth. IZA DP No. 8157. April. Updated in Roine, J., and D. Waldenström (2015) "Long-run trends in the distribution of income and wealth", In: Atkinson, A.B., Bourguignon, F. (Eds.), Handbook of Income Distribution, vol. 2A, North-Holland, Amsterdam. pp. 469–592

[b]L. Soltow (1989) Distribution of Wealth and Income in the United States in 1798. University of Pittsburgh Press

(continued)

[c]Piketty (2014) Capital in the 21st Century. Chapter 10. Table 10.1
[d]Osberg, Lars (1984) Economic Inequality in the United States. M.E. Sharpe, Inc. New York and London. Notes: 1962 is Wealth from consumer units. 1973 is family net worth
[e]Chartbook of Economic Inequality. (Accessed January 2016). http://www.chartbookofeconomicinequality.com/
[f]Alice Hanson Jones, Wealth of a Nation to Be (1980), Tables 6.1, 8.2, 8.3, 8.8, and 8.10
[g]Carole Shammas (1993) "A New Look at Long-Term Trends in Inequality" American Historical Review
[h]Pfeffer et al. (2013). PSID-Panel Study of Income Dynamics
[i]Davies et al. (2011) Table 7, p. 246
[j]Gallman (1969, Table 1. P. 6)
[k]Saez and Zucman (2016) Table B1. Total Net Household Wealth

# Appendix 4

## *Estimates of Wealth Inequality for the United Kingdom, 1668–2013*

| | *Year* | *Gini* | *Top 1 percent* | *Top 10 percent* |
|---|---|---|---|---|
| United Kingdom[a] | 1740 | | | 86.0 |
| | 1810 | | | 83.4 |
| | 1875 | | | 83.8 |
| | 1911 | | | 92.0 |
| | 1923 | | | 89.1 |
| | 1924 | | | 88.1 |
| | 1925 | | | 88.4 |
| | 1926 | | | 87.4 |
| | 1927 | | | 88.3 |
| | 1928 | | | 87.2 |
| | 1929 | | | 86.3 |
| | 1930 | | | 86.6 |
| | 1936 | | | 85.7 |
| | 1938 | | | 85.0 |
| | 1960 | | | 71.5 |
| | 1961 | | | 71.7 |
| | 1962 | | | 67.3 |

*(continued)*

(continued)

| *Year* | *Gini* | *Top 1 percent* | *Top 10 percent* |
|---|---|---|---|
| 1964 | | | 71.4 |
| 1965 | | | 71.7 |
| 1966 | | | 69.2 |
| 1967 | | | 70.0 |
| 1968 | | | 71.6 |
| 1969 | | | 67.7 |
| 1970 | | | 68.7 |
| 1971 | | | 67.6 |
| 1972 | | | 70.4 |
| 1976 | | | 50.0 |
| 1977 | | | 50.0 |
| 1978 | | | 49.0 |
| 1979 | | | 50.0 |
| 1980 | | | 50.0 |
| 1981 | | | 50.0 |
| 1982 | | | 49.0 |
| 1983 | | | 50.0 |
| 1984 | | | 48.0 |
| 1985 | | | 49.0 |
| 1986 | | | 50.0 |
| 1987 | | | 51.0 |
| 1988 | | | 49.0 |
| 1989 | | | 48.0 |
| 1990 | | | 47.0 |
| 1991 | | | 47.0 |
| 1992 | | | 50.0 |
| 1993 | | | 51.0 |
| 1994 | | | 52.0 |
| 1995 | | | 50.0 |
| 1996 | | | 52.0 |
| 1997 | | | 54.0 |
| 1998 | | | 52.0 |
| 1999 | | | 55.0 |
| 2000 | | | 56.0 |
| 2001 | | | 54.0 |
| 2002 | | | 54.0 |
| 2003 | | | 53.0 |
| 2005 | | | 54.0 |

(*continued*)

(continued)

| | *Year* | *Gini* | *Top 1 percent* | *Top 10 percent* |
|---|---|---|---|---|
| United Kingdom[b] | 1668 | 0.807 | 28.1 | 76.3 |
| | 1669 | 0.807 | 37.9 | 73.6 |
| | 1670 | 0.793 | 21.9 | 67.4 |
| | 1698 | 0.859 | 13.0 | 80.5 |
| | 1699 | 0.811 | 27.9 | 74.8 |
| | 1700 | 0.761 | 31.0 | 65.4 |
| | 1729 | 0.675 | 10.9 | 55.1 |
| | 1730 | 0.668 | 17.8 | 58.7 |
| | 1731 | 0.613 | 12.1 | 44.6 |
| | 1738 | 0.765 | 11.0 | 64.3 |
| | 1739 | 0.838 | 38.9 | 77.8 |
| | 1740 | 0.816 | 28.2 | 72.6 |
| | 1741 | 0.737 | 13.9 | 65.3 |
| | 1810 | 0.789 | 23.2 | 69.9 |
| | 1875 | 0.816 | 27.8 | 73.5 |
| United Kingdom[c] | 1966 | 0.810 | | 69.0 |
| | 1976 | 0.760 | | 60.0 |
| | 1985 | 0.650 | | 49.0 |
| | 1993 | 0.650 | | 48.0 |
| United Kingdom[d] | 2006 | 0.610 | | 43.9 |
| | 2008 | 0.610 | | 43.6 |
| | 2010 | 0.610 | | 43.7 |
| United Kingdom[e] | 1976 | 0.660 | | 50.0 |
| | 1981 | 0.650 | | 50.0 |
| | 1986 | 0.640 | | 50.0 |
| | 1991 | 0.640 | | 47.0 |
| | 1996 | 0.680 | | 52.0 |
| | 2001 | 0.680 | | 54.0 |
| | 2005 | 0.700 | | 54.0 |
| United Kingdom[f] | 1923 | | 41.8 | |
| | 1924 | | 41.2 | |
| | 1925 | | 41.9 | |
| | 1926 | | 39.4 | |
| | 1927 | | 41.1 | |
| | 1928 | | 39.2 | |
| | 1929 | | 38.1 | |
| | 1930 | | 39.8 | |
| | 1936 | | 37.2 | |
| | 1937 | | 37.8 | |
| | 1950 | | 32.4 | |
| | 1951 | | 31.5 | |

(*continued*)

(continued)

| *Year* | *Gini* | *Top 1 percent* | *Top 10 percent* |
|---|---|---|---|
| 1952 | | 29.5 | |
| 1953 | | 29.9 | |
| 1954 | | 31.1 | |
| 1955 | | 30.1 | |
| 1956 | | 30.2 | |
| 1957 | | 29.5 | |
| 1958 | | 28.1 | |
| 1959 | | 28.7 | |
| 1960 | | 29.4 | |
| 1961 | | 31.2 | |
| 1962 | | 27.2 | |
| 1964 | | 29.6 | |
| 1965 | | 28.4 | |
| 1966 | | 26.5 | |
| 1967 | | 26.9 | |
| 1968 | | 28.7 | |
| 1969 | | 26.7 | |
| 1970 | | 25.7 | |
| 1971 | | 24.6 | |
| 1972 | | 27.3 | |
| 1973 | | 23.4 | |
| 1974 | | 19.5 | |
| 1975 | | 19.7 | |
| 1976 | | 21.0 | |
| 1977 | | 22.0 | |
| 1978 | | 20.0 | |
| 1979 | | 20.0 | |
| 1980 | | 19.0 | |
| 1981 | | 18.0 | |
| 1982 | | 18.0 | |
| 1983 | | 20.0 | |
| 1984 | | 18.0 | |
| 1985 | | 18.0 | |
| 1986 | | 18.0 | |
| 1987 | | 18.0 | |
| 1988 | | 17.0 | |
| 1989 | | 17.0 | |
| 1990 | | 18.0 | |
| 1991 | | 17.0 | |
| 1992 | | 18.0 | |
| 1993 | | 18.0 | |
| 1994 | | 19.0 | |

(*continued*)

(continued)

| | Year | Gini | Top 1 percent | Top 10 percent |
|---|---|---|---|---|
| | 1995 | | 19.0 | |
| | 1996 | | 20.0 | |
| | 1997 | | 22.0 | |
| | 1998 | | 22.0 | |
| | 1999 | | 23.0 | |
| | 2000 | | 23.0 | |
| | 2001 | | 22.0 | |
| | 2002 | | 21.0 | |
| | 2003 | | 19.0 | |
| | 2005 | | 21.0 | |
| United Kingdom[g] | 1870 | 0.863 | | |
| | 1902 | 0.863 | | |
| United Kingdom[h] | 2000 | 0.697 | | |
| United Kingdom[i] | 1810 | | 54.9 | 82.9 |
| | 1870 | | 61.1 | 87.1 |
| | 1910 | | 69.0 | 92.0 |
| | 1920 | | 61.0 | 89.0 |
| | 1930 | | 55.0 | 85.0 |
| | 1950 | | 47.2 | 76.0 |
| | 1960 | | 33.9 | 71.5 |
| | 1970 | | 22.6 | 64.1 |
| | 1980 | | 22.7 | 62.6 |
| | 1990 | | 24.0 | 64.0 |
| | 2000 | | 27.0 | 68.5 |
| United Kingdom[j] | 2010 | | 28.0 | 70.5 |
| | 1895 | | 69.2 | 96.5 |
| | 1896 | | 69.7 | 96.4 |
| | 1897 | | 70.6 | 96.2 |
| | 1898 | | 69.4 | 96.1 |
| | 1899 | | 70.6 | 96.0 |
| | 1900 | | 69.9 | 96.1 |
| | 1901 | | 73.0 | 96.4 |
| | 1902 | | 69.9 | 96.0 |
| | 1903 | | 69.6 | 95.8 |
| | 1904 | | 69.2 | 95.8 |
| | 1905 | | 70.6 | 96.0 |
| | 1906 | | 71.3 | 96.0 |
| | 1907 | | 69.2 | 95.6 |
| | 1908 | | 67.9 | 95.5 |
| | 1909 | | 69.5 | 95.6 |
| | 1910 | | 68.1 | 95.3 |
| | 1911 | | 67.9 | 95.2 |
| | 1912 | | 67.8 | 95.2 |

(*continued*)

(continued)

| | *Year* | *Gini* | *Top 1 percent* | *Top 10 percent* |
|---|---|---|---|---|
| | 1913 | | 66.7 | 95.0 |
| | 1914 | | 67.3 | 95.1 |
| | 1919 | | 61.8 | 91.7 |
| | 1920 | | 60.1 | 91.7 |
| | 1921 | | 59.8 | 91.3 |
| | 1922 | | 61.0 | 92.0 |
| | 1923 | | 59.6 | 91.7 |
| | 1924 | | 59.3 | 91.6 |
| | 1925 | | 58.2 | 91.4 |
| | 1926 | | 56.6 | 90.8 |
| | 1927 | | 56.7 | 91.1 |
| | 1928 | | 57.4 | 90.8 |
| | 1929 | | 56.3 | 90.5 |
| | 1930 | | 56.8 | 89.9 |
| | 1931 | | 52.4 | 88.8 |
| | 1932 | | 53.6 | 88.7 |
| | 1933 | | 55.3 | 89.4 |
| | 1934 | | 53.1 | 89.1 |
| | 1935 | | 53.3 | 88.9 |
| | 1936 | | 52.9 | 88.8 |
| | 1937 | | 52.5 | 88.4 |
| | 1938 | | 49.9 | 87.2 |
| | 1939 | | 50.5 | 87.2 |
| | 1940 | | 50.3 | 86.7 |
| | 1941 | | 49.2 | 85.6 |
| | 1946 | | 45.4 | 86.3 |
| | 1947 | | 44.3 | 85.8 |
| | 1948 | | 43.8 | 85.9 |
| | 1949 | | 42.8 | 84.5 |
| | 1950 | | 40.8 | 82.5 |
| | 1951 | | 39.3 | 80.8 |
| | 1952 | | 38.3 | 79.9 |
| | 1953 | | 38.6 | 79.3 |
| | 1954 | | 38.6 | 79.0 |
| | 1955 | | 37.7 | 77.6 |
| | 1956 | | 36.0 | 76.1 |
| | 1957 | | 35.4 | 74.5 |
| | 1958 | | 34.2 | 74.1 |
| | 1959 | | 34.7 | 73.7 |
| | 1960 | | 33.7 | 73.0 |
| | 1961 | | 33.2 | 72.0 |
| | 1962 | | 31.8 | 70.5 |

(*continued*)

(continued)

| *Year* | *Gini* | *Top 1 percent* | *Top 10 percent* |
|---|---|---|---|
| 1963 | | 32.0 | 70.0 |
| 1964 | | 31.7 | 70.7 |
| 1965 | | 29.8 | 69.9 |
| 1966 | | 28.6 | 68.8 |
| 1967 | | 28.9 | 68.4 |
| 1968 | | 29.8 | 69.0 |
| 1969 | | 28.4 | 67.0 |
| 1970 | | 26.1 | 65.2 |
| 1971 | | 26.6 | 64.8 |
| 1972 | | 27.3 | 67.3 |
| 1973 | | 24.1 | 63.7 |
| 1974 | | 22.6 | 61.7 |
| 1975 | | 21.4 | 58.2 |
| 1976 | | 21.1 | 60.0 |
| 1977 | | 20.5 | 57.7 |
| 1978 | | 19.2 | 56.8 |
| 1979 | | 18.7 | 55.2 |
| 1980 | | 16.7 | 52.3 |
| 1981 | | 16.9 | 52.0 |
| 1982 | | 16.9 | 52.1 |
| 1983 | | 17.1 | 51.8 |
| 1984 | | 16.1 | 48.7 |
| 1985 | | 17.4 | 51.1 |
| 1986 | | 16.7 | 50.8 |
| 1987 | | 18.0 | 52.6 |
| 1988 | | 16.2 | 49.3 |
| 1989 | | 17.7 | 49.3 |
| 1990 | | 15.8 | 46.6 |
| 1991 | | 15.7 | 46.5 |
| 1992 | | 17.4 | 49.1 |
| 1993 | | 18.8 | 51.4 |
| 1994 | | 18.3 | 51.1 |
| 1996 | | 18.9 | 52.6 |
| 1997 | | 20.4 | 54.9 |
| 1998 | | 19.5 | 52.6 |
| 1999 | | 18.5 | 51.5 |
| 2000 | | 19.4 | 51.7 |
| 2001 | | 18.6 | 51.0 |
| 2002 | | 16.8 | 49.4 |
| 2003 | | 15.8 | 48.1 |
| 2005 | | 15.7 | 48.2 |
| 2006 | | 15.6 | 46.9 |

(*continued*)

(continued)

| Year | Gini | Top 1 percent | Top 10 percent |
|---|---|---|---|
| 2007 | | 16.1 | 46.9 |
| 2008 | | 16.4 | 48.3 |
| 2009 | | 15.2 | 46.2 |
| 2010 | | 16.3 | 48.3 |
| 2011 | | 16.5 | 47.4 |
| 2012 | | 16.1 | 47.1 |
| 2013 | | 16.2 | 47.3 |

Notes

[a]Source: Roine and Waldenstrom (2014) Tables A1–A4, Roine and Waldenstrom (2014) Long-Run Trends in the Distribution of Income and Wealth. IZA DP No. 8157. April, pp. 469–592. Updated in Roine, J., and D. Waldenström (2015) "Long-run trends in the distribution of income and wealth", In: Atkinson, A.B., Bourguignon, F. (Eds.), Handbook of Income Distribution, vol. 2A, North-Holland, Amsterdam.
[b]Lindert Probate Data. English Probates 1670–1875. http://economics.ucdavis.edu/people/fzlinder/peter-linderts-webpage/data-and-estimates/english-probates-1670-1875
[c]Davies and Shorrocks (1999) Chapter 11: The distribution of Wealth in Handbook of Income Distribution: Volume 1. Edited by A. B. Atkinson and F Bourguignon
[d]Wealth Inequality the Facts. Institute for Economic Affairs. http://www.iea.org.uk/sites/default/files/publications/files/Wealth%20inequality%20briefing%20formatted.pdf
[e]Wealth Inequality: Key facts. Karen Rowlingson. December 2012. University of Birmingham. Policy Commission on the distribution of Wealth. http://www.birmingham.ac.uk/Documents/research/SocialSciences/Key-Facts-Background-Paper-BPCIV.pdf
[f]Chartbook of Economic Inequality. (Accessed January 2016). http://www.chartbookofeconomicinequality.com/
[g]Di Matteo, L., D. Green, A. Owens, M. Shanahan, J. McAloon (2012) Resources, land abundance and inequality. Understanding wealth-holding and investment in Britain and its settler colonies, 1870–1930, SSHA Meetings Vancouver, November 1–4
[h]Davies et al. (2011) Table 7, p. 246
[i]Piketty (2014) Fig. 10.5
[j]Alvaredo et al. (2017)

# Appendix 5

## *Local Polynomial Smoothing for the United Kingdom Under Alternate Assumption*

Wealth Share of Top 10 Percent, Outlier Adjusted (Wealth Shares Under 59 Percent Dropped).

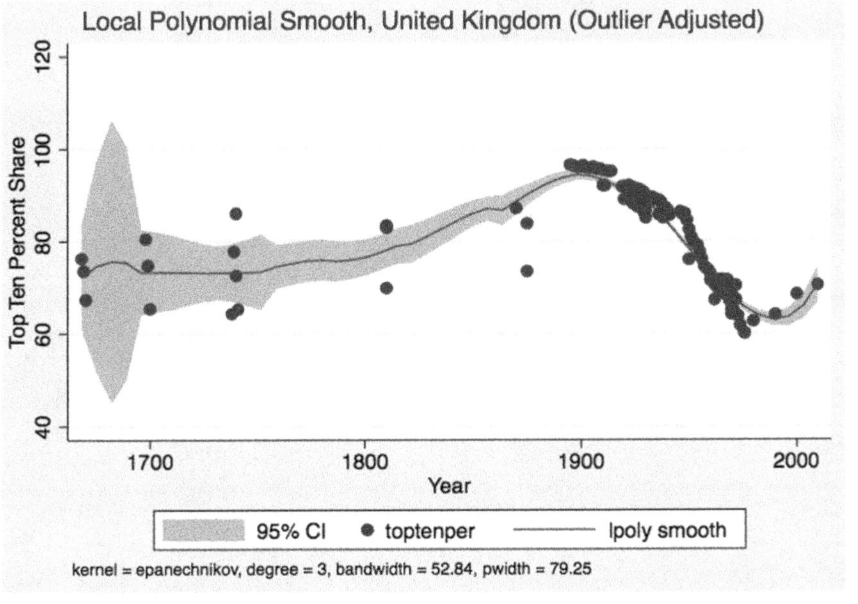

# References


Abad, L. A., & Junquera, P. A. (2017). Latin American Earnings Inequality in the Long Run. *Cliometrica, 11*(3), 349–374.

Alfani, G. (2015). Economic Inequality in Northwestern Italy: A Long-Term View (Fourteenth to Eighteenth Centuries). *Journal of Economic History, 75*(4), 1058–1096.

Alfani, G. (2017). The Rich in Historical Perspective: Evidence for Preindustrial Europe (ca. 1300–1800). *Cliometrica, 11*(3), 321–348.

Alfani, G., & Ammannati, F. (2017). Long-Term Trends in Economic Inequality: The Case of the Florentine State, c. 1300–1800. *The Economic History Review, 70*(4), 1072–1102.

Alfani, G., & Ryckbosch, W. (2016). Growing Apart in Early Modern Europe? A Comparison of Inequality Trends in Italy and the Low Countries, 1500–1800. *Explorations in Economic History, 62*, 143–153.

Alston, L. J., & Schapiro, M. O. (1984). Inheritance Laws Across Colonies: Causes and Consequences. *Journal of Economic History, 44*(2), 277–287.

Alvaredo, F., Atkinson, A. B., & Morelli, S. (2017, January). *Top Wealth Shares in the UK over More than a Century*. Centre for Studies in Economics and Finance, Working Paper No. 464.

Ando, A., & Modigliani, F. (1963). The 'Life-Cycle' Hypothesis of Saving: Aggregate Implications and Tests. *American Economic Review, 53*, 55–84.

Armour, P., Burkhauser, R. V., & Larrimore, J. (2013). Deconstructing Income Inequality Measures: A Crosswalk from Market Income to Comprehensive Income. *American Economic Review: Papers and Proceedings, 103*(3), 173–177.




L. Di Matteo, *The Evolution and Determinants of Wealth Inequality in the North Atlantic Anglo-Sphere, 1668–2013*,
https://doi.org/10.1007/978-3-319-89773-8

Arrondel, L., & Grange, C. (2003). The Accumulation and Transmission of Wealth over Long Periods: Example of a Rural Family from Loire-Atlantique in the 19th and 20th Centuries. *The History of the Family: An International Quarterly, 2003*(8), 103–134.

Arrondel, L., & Grange, C. (2006). Transmission and Inequality of Wealth: An Empirical Study of Wealth Mobility from 1800 to 1938 in France. *Journal of Economic Inequality, 2006*(4), 209–232.

Arrondel, L., & Grange, C. (2014). Bequests and Family Traditions: The Case of Nineteenth Century France. *Review of Economics of the Household, 12*(3), 439–459.

Ashton, T. S. (1961/1948). *The Industrial Revolution*. London: Oxford University Press.

Atack, J., & Bateman, F. (1981). Egalitarianism, Inequality, and Age: The Rural North in 1860. *Journal of Economic History, XLI*, 85–93.

Atack, J., & Passell, P. (1994). *A New Economic View of American History: From Colonial Times to 1940* (2nd ed.). New York: Norton.

Atkinson, A. B. (2000). Distribution of Income and Wealth in Britain over the Twentieth Century. In A. Halsey & J. Webb (Eds.), *Twentieth-Century British Social Trends*. Basingstoke: Palgrave Macmillan.

Atkinson, A. B. (2013, November). *Wealth and Inheritance in Britain from 1896 to the Present*. Centre for Analysis of Social Exclusion, No. 173.

Atkinson, A. B., & Brandolini, A. (2001). Promise and Pitfalls in the Use of "Secondary" Data-Sets: Income Inequality in OECD Countries as a Case Study. *Journal of Economic Literature, 39*(3), 771–799.

Atkinson, A. B., & Harrison, A. (1978). *The Distribution of Personal Wealth in Britain*. Cambridge: Cambridge University Press.

Atkinson, A. B., Gordon, J. P. F., & Harrison, A. (1989). Trends in the Shares of Top Wealthholders in Britain: 1923–1989. *Oxford Bulletin of Economics and Statistics, 51*(3), 315–332.

Baldwin, J. R., & MacDonald, R. (2012). *Natural Resources, the Terms of Trade, and Real Income Growth in Canada: 1870 to 2010*. Statistics Canada, Economic Analysis (EA) Research Paper Series, No. 11F0027M—No. 7.

Barro, R. J. (2000). Inequality and Growth in a Panel of Countries. *Journal of Economic Growth, 5*, 5–32.

Barro, R. J. (2008). *Inequality and Growth Revisited*. ADB Working Paper on Regional Economic Integration No. 11.

Baskerville, P. (1999). Women and Investment in Late-Nineteenth-Urban Canada: Victoria and Hamilton, 1880–1901. *The Canadian Historical Review, 80*(2), 191–218.

Bengtsson, E., Missiaia, A., Olsson, M., & Svenson, P. (2016, November). *The Wealth of the Richest: Inequality and the Nobility in Sweden, 1750–1900*. Paper Presented at the Social Science History Meetings, Chicago.

Bennett, J. C. (2007). *The Anglosphere Challenge. Why English-Speaking Nations Will Lead the Way in the Twenty-First Century*. New York: Rowman and Littlefield.

Bernheim, B. D., Shleifer, A., & Summers, L. H. (1985). The Strategic Bequest Motive. *Journal of Political Economy, 93*(6), 1045–1076. https://doi.org/10.1086/261351.

Bird, R. (1978). Canada's Vanishing Death Taxes. *Osgoode Hall Law Journal, 16*(1), 133–145.

Boadway, R., Chamberlain, E., & Emmerson, C. (2009). *Taxation of Wealth and Wealth Transfers: Appendices*. Prepared for the Report of a commission on Reforming the Tax System for the 21st Century, Chaired by Sir James Mirrlees, The Institute for Fiscal Studies. www.ofs.org.uk/mirrleesreview

Bolton, S. C. (1982). Inequality on the Southern Frontier: Arkansas County in the Arkansas Territory. *The Arkansas Historical Quarterly, 41*(1), 51–66.

Bouchard, G. (1998). Economic Inequalities in Saguenay Society, 1879–1949: A Descriptive Analysis. *The Canadian Historical Review, 79*(4), 660–690.

Bricker, J., Henriques, A., Krimmel, J., & Sabelhaus, J. (2016). Estimating Top Income and Wealth Shares: Sensitivity to Data and Methods. *American Economic Review: Papers and Proceedings, 106*(5), 641–645.

Broadberry, S. (2015). *British Economic Growth, 1270–1870*. Cambridge: Cambridge University Press.

Burchell, R. A. (1987). Opportunity and the Frontier: Wealth-Holding in Twenty-Six Northern Californian Counties 1848–1880. *The Western Historical Quarterly, 18*(2), 177–196.

Burkhauser, R. V., Hahn, M., & Wilkins, R. (2013). *Measuring Top Incomes Using Tax Record Data: A Cautionary Tale from Australia*. NBER Working Paper No. 19121.

Canaday, N. (2008). The Accumulation of Property by Southern Blacks and Whites: Individual-Level Evidence from a South Carolina Cotton County, 1910–1919. *Explorations in Economic History, 45*, 51–75.

Card, D., Lemieux, T., & Riddell, C. (2004). Unions and Wage Inequality. *Journal of Labour Research, 25*(4), 519–559.

Castagnoli, E., & Muliere, P. (1990). A Note on Inequality Measures and The Pigou-Dalton Principle of Transfers. In C. Dagum & M. Zenga (Eds.), *Income and Wealth Distribution, Inequality and Poverty*. Berlin: Springer, 1710182.

Clay, K., & Jones, R. (2008). Migrating to Riches? Evidence from the California Gold Rush. *The Journal of Economic History, 68*(4), 997–1027.

Cleveland, W. S. (1979). Robust Locally Weighted Regression and Smoothing Scatterplots. *Journal of the American Statistical Association, 74*, 829–836.

Cleveland, W. S. (1985). *The Elements of Graphing*. Monterey: Wadsworth.

Cleveland, W. S. (1993). *Visualizing Data*. Summit: Hobart.

Coatsworth, J. H. (2008). Inequality, Institutions and Economic Growth in Latin America. *Journal of Latin American Studies, 40*(August), 545–569.

Congression Budget Office. (2009, December 18). *Federal Estate and Gift Taxes.* Economic and Business Issue Brief.

Cowell, F. A. (2009, December). Measuring Inequality. http://darp.lse.ac.uk/papersDB/Cowell_measuringinequality3.pdf

Daly, M. (2016). *Killing the Competition: Economic Inequality and Homicide.* New York: Routledge.

Darroch, G. (1983). Early Industrialization and Inequality in Toronto, 1861–1899. *Labour/Le Travailleur, 11*, 31–61.

Darroch, G., & Soltow, L. (1994). *Property and Inequality in Victorian Ontario Structural Patterns and Cultural Communities in the 1871 Census.* Toronto: University of Toronto Press.

Davies, J. B. (1979). On the Size Distribution of Wealth in Canada. *Review of Income and Wealth, 25*(3), 237–259.

Davies, J. B., & Di Matteo, L. (2017). *Filling the Gap: Examining Canadian Wealth Inequality Over the Long Run.* Paper Prepared for Presentation at the 51st Annual Meetings of the Canadian Economic Association, Antigonish, Nova Scotia. Manuscript.

Davies, J. B., & Shorrocks, A. F. (1999). The Distribution of Wealth. In A. B. Atkinson & F. Bourguignon (Eds.), *Handbook of Income Distribution* (Vol. 1). New York: Elsevier Science.

Davies, J. B., Sandstrom, S., Shorrocks, A., & Wolff, E. N. (2011). The Level and Distribution of Global Household Wealth. *The Economic Journal, 121*, 223–254.

Deininger, K., & Squire, L. (1998). New Ways of Looking at Old Issues: Inequality and Growth. *Journal of Development Economics, 57*, 259–287.

Delong, B. (2003). Bequests: An Historical Perspective. In A. H. Munnell & A. Sundén (Eds.), *Death and Dollars: The Role of Gifts and Bequests in America, Chapter 2.* Washington, DC: Brookings Institution Press.

Di Matteo, L. (1996). The Wealth of the Irish in Nineteenth Century Ontario. *Social Science History, 20*(2), 209–234.

Di Matteo, L. (1997). The Determinants of Wealth and Asset Holding in Nineteenth Century Canada: Evidence from Micro-data. *Journal of Economic History, 57*(4), 907–934.

Di Matteo, L. (1998). Wealth Accumulation and the Life-Cycle in Economic History: Implications of Alternative Approaches to Data. *Explorations in Economic History, 35*(3), 296–324. *Erratum, 36*(1), 107.

Di Matteo, L. (2001). Patterns and Determinants of Wealth Inequality in Late-Nineteenth Century Ontario. *Social Science History, 25*(3), 347–380.

Di Matteo, L. (2004). Resource Boom and Bust, 1885–1920: Regional Wealth Evidence from Probate Records. *Australian Economic History Review, 44*(1), 52–78.

Di Matteo, L. (2012). Land and Inequality in Canada 1870–1930. *Scandinavian Economic History Review, 60*(3), 309–334.

Di Matteo, L. (2013a). Women, Wealth and Economic Change: An Assessment of the Impact of Women's Property Law in Wentworth County, Ontario, 1872–1927. *Explorations in Economic History, 50*, 285–307.

Di Matteo, L. (2013b). *Measuring Government in the 21st Century: An International Overview of the Size and Efficiency of Public Spending*. Vancouver: Fraser Institute.

Di Matteo, L. (2016a). Wealth Distribution and the Canadian Middle Class: Historical Evidence and Policy Implications. *Canadian Public Policy, 42*(2), 132–151.

Di Matteo, L. (2016b). All Equal in the Sight of God: Economic Inequality and Religion in the Early Twentieth Century. *European Review of Economic History, 20*, 23–45.

Di Matteo, L. (2017a). Does Egalitarianism Come at a Price? Inequality and Economic Performance in Late Nineteenth Century Ontario. *Social Science History, 41*, 1–30.

Di Matteo, L. (2017b). Major Changes to the Federal Personal Income Tax: 1917–2017. In W. Watson & J. Clemens (Eds.), *Zero to 50 in 100 Years: The History and Development of Canada's Personal Income Tax*. Vancouver: Fraser Institute.

Di Matteo, L., & George, P. (1992). Canadian Wealth Inequality in the Late Nineteenth Century: A Study of Wentworth County, Ontario, 1872–1902. *The Canadian Historical Review, LXXIII*, 453–483.

Di Matteo, L., & George, P. (1998). Patterns and Determinants of Wealth Among Probated Decedents in Wentworth County, Ontario, 1872–1902. *Histoire Sociale/Social History, XXXI*(61), 1–34.

Disney, R., & Luo, G. (2014). *The Right to Buy Public Housing in Britain: A Welfare Analysis*. (Working paper W15/05). Institute for Fiscal Studies.

Dupont, B., & Rosenblook, J. (2016, April). *The Impact of the Civil War on Southern Wealth Holders*. NBER Working Paper No. 22184.

Engerman, S. L., & Gallman, R. E. (1996). *The Cambridge Economic History of the United States. Volume I. The Colonial Era*. Cambridge: Cambridge University Press.

Engerman, S. L., & Gallman, R. E. (2000a). *The Cambridge Economic History of the United StatesVolume II. The Long Nineteenth Century*. Cambridge: Cambridge University Press.

Engerman, S. L., & Gallman, R. E. (2000b). *The Cambridge Economic History of the United States. Volume III. The Twentieth Century.* Cambridge: Cambridge University Press.

Ferrie, J. (1994). The Wealth Accumulation of Antebellum European Immigrants to the U.S., 1840–1860. *Journal of Economic History, 54,* 1–33.

Firestone, O. J. (1960). *Canada's External Trade and Net Foreign Balance, 1851–1900.* Trends in the American Economy in the Nineteenth Century, The Conference on Research in Income and Wealth, Princeton University Press, pp. 757–771. http://www.nber.org/chapters/c11719

Fisher, J., Johnson, D., Smeeding, T., & Thompson, J. (2016a, September). *Inequality in 3D: Income, Consumption and Wealth. Washington Center for Equitable Growth* (Working Paper Series).

Fisher, J., Johnson, D., Latner, J. P., Smeeding, T., & Thompson, J. (2016b). Inequality and Mobility Using Income, Consumption, and Wealth for the Same Individuals. *The Russell Sage Foundation Journal of the Social Sciences, 2,* 44–58.

Floud, R., & Johnson, P. (Eds.). (2004). *The Cambridge Economic History of Modern Britain. Volume 1. Industrialization, 1700–1860.* Cambridge: Cambridge University Press.

Floud, R., & Johnson, P. (Eds.). (2008). *The Cambridge Economic History of Modern Britain. Volume 2. Economic Maturity, 1860 to 1939.* Cambridge: Cambridge University Press.

Freund, C., & Oliver, S. (2016). *The Origins of the Superrich: The Billionaire Characteristics Database, Working Paper Series* (Vol. 16-1). Washington, DC: Peterson Institute for International Economics.

Gagan, D. (1976). The Indivisibility of Land: A Micro-analysis of the System of Inheritance in Nineteenth Century Ontario. *Journal of Economic History, 36,* 126–141.

Galarneau, D., & Sohn, T. (2013). *Long-Term Trends in Unionization.* Statistics Canada, Insights on Canadian Society. 75-006-X. http://www.statcan.gc.ca/pub/75-006-x/2013001/article/11878-eng.pdf

Gallman, R. E. (1969). Trends in the Size Distribution of Wealth in the Nineteenth Century: Some Speculations. In L. Soltow (Ed.), *Six Papers on the Size Distribution of Wealth and Income.* New York: National Bureau of Economic Research.

Gallman, R. E. (1978). Professor Pessen on the 'Egalitarian Myth'. *Social Science History, 2,* 194–207.

Gallup, J. L. (2012). *Is There a Kuznets Curve?* Working Paper. https://www.pdx.edu/econ/sites/www.pdx.edu.econ/files/kuznets_complete.pdf

Galt, M. N. (1985). Wealth and Income in New Zealand 1870 to 1939. Unpublished PhD Thesis, Victoria University, Wellington

Garbinti, B., Goupille-Lebret, J., & Piketty, T. (2016). *Accounting for Wealth Inequality Dynamics: Methods, Estimates and Simulations for France (1800–2014)*. World Wealth and Income Database, Working Paper No. 2016/5.

Goodman, W. D. (1995). Death Taxes in Canada, in the Past and in the Possible Future. *Canadian Tax Journal, 43*(5), 1360–1376.

Gordon, R. J. (2016). *The Rise and Fall of American Growth*. Princeton: Princeton University Press.

Green, A. G. (1967). Regional Aspects of Canada's Economic Growth, 1890–1929. *The Canadian Journal of Economics, 33*(2), 232–245.

Green, A. G. (1968/1969). Regional Inequality, Structural Change, and Economic Growth in Canada. *Economic Development and Cultural Change, 17*, 567–583.

Green, A. G. (1971). *Regional Aspects of Canadian Economic Growth*. Toronto: University of Toronto Press.

Gregson, M. E. (1996). Wealth Accumulation and Distribution in the Midwest in the Late Nineteenth Century. *Explorations in Economic History, 33*, 524–538.

Gwyn, J., & Siddiq, F. K. (1992). Wealth Distribution in Nova Scotia During the Confederation Era, 1851 and 1871. *Canadian Historical Review, LXXIII*(4), 435–452.

Hamilton, G. C., Keay, I., & Lewis, F. (2017). Contributions to Canadian Economic History: The Last 30 Years. *Canadian Journal of Economics, 50*(5), 1632–1657.

Hardle, W. (1991). *Applied Nonparametric Regression, Econometric Society Monographs* (Vol. 19). Cambridge: Cambridge University Press.

Herscovici, S. (1993). The Distribution of Wealth in Nineteenth Century Boston: Inequality Among Natives and Immigrants, 1860. *Explorations in Economic History, 30*, 321–335.

Higgins, M., & Williamson, J. G. (2002). Explaining Inequality the World Round: Cohort Size, Kuznets Curves, and Openness. *Southeast Asian Studies, 40*(3), 268–302. Reprinted in B. Milanovic (Ed.) (2012). *Globalization and Inequality*. Cheltenham: Elgar.

Innis, H. A. (1930). The Importance of Staple Products. In W. T. Easterbrook & M. H. Watkins (Eds.), *Approaches to Canadian Economic History*. Toronto: McClelland and Stewart, 1967.

Jackson, A. (2015, April 8). *The Return of the Gilded Age: Consequences, Causes and Solutions*. Broadbent Institute, The Harry Kitchen Lecture in Public Policy.

Johnson, B. W., & Eller, M. B. (1998). Federal Taxation of Inheritance and Wealth Transfers. In R. K. Miller & S. J. McNamee (Eds.), *Inheritance and Wealth in America* (pp. 61–90). New York: Plenum Press.

Johnson, L. L., & Frank, Z. (2006). Cities and Wealth in the South Atlantic: Buenos Aires and Riode Janeiro Before 1860. *Comparative Studies in Society and History, 48*(3), 634–668.

Jones, A. H. (1980). *Wealth of A Nation to Be: The American Colonies on the Eve of the Revolution*. New York: Columbia Press.

Keay, I. (2007). The Engine or the Caboose? Resource Industries and Twentieth-Century Canadian Economic Performance. *The Journal of Economic History, 67*(1), 1–32.

Kennickell, A. (2009). *Ponds and Streams: Wealth and Income in the U.S., 1989 to 2007*. Finance and Economics Discussion Series 2009-13, Board of Governors of the Federal Reserve System (U.S.).

Kennickell, A. (2011). *Tossed and Turned: Wealth Dynamics of U.S. Households 2007–2009*. Finance and Economics Discussion Series 2011-51, Board of Governors of the Federal Reserve System (U.S.).

Kenny, M., & Pearce, N. (2015, February 10). *The Rise of the Anglosphere: How the Right Dreamed Up a New World Order*. New Statesman. http://www.newstatesman.com/politics/2015/02/rise-anglosphere-how-right-dreamed-new-conservative-world-order

King, R. (2012). *Theories and Typologies of Migration: An Overview and A Primer*. Willy Brandt Working Papers in International Migration and Ethnic Relations, Malmo University, 3/12.

Kopczuk, W., & Saez, E. (2004). Top Wealth Shares in the United States, 1916–2000: Evidence from Estate Tax Returns. *National Tax Journal, 57*(2), 445–487.

Krueger, D., & Perri, F. (2006). Does Income Inequality Lead to Consumption Equality? Evidence and Theory. *Review of Economic Studies, 73*(1), 163–193.

Kuznets, S. (1955). Economic Growth and Income Inequality. *American Economic Review, XLV*(1), 1–28.

Kuznets, S. (1966). *Modern Economic Growth Rate, Structure and Spread*. New Haven: Yale University Press.

Landy, B. (2013, August 28). *A Tale of Two Recoveries: Wealth Inequality After the Great Recession*. The Century Foundation. Issue Brief. https://tcf.org/content/commentary/a-tale-of-two-recoveries-wealth-inequality-after-the-great-recession/

Lee, E. S. (1966). A Theory of Migration. *Demography, 3*(1), 47–57.

Lemon, J. T. (1972). *The Best Poor Man's Country: A Geographical Study of Early Southeastern Pennsylvania*. Baltimore: John Hopkins Press.

Lewis, S. (2010, April 30). How Union Membership Has Grown—And Shrunk. *The Guardian*. https://www.theguardian.com/news/datablog/2010/apr/30/union-membership-data#data

Lindert, P. H. (1986). Unequal English Wealth Since 1670. *The Journal of Political Economy, 94*(6), 1127–1162.

Lindert, P. H. (1991). Toward a Comparative History of Income and Wealth. In Y. S. Brenner, H. Kaelble, & M. Thomas (Eds.), *Income Distribution in Historical Perspective* (pp. 212–231). Cambridge: Cambridge University Press.

Lindert, P. H. (2000). Three Centuries of Inequality in Britain and America. In A. B. Atkinson & F. Bourguignon (Eds.), *Handbook of Income Distribution* (Vol. 1). Amsterdam: North-Holland.

Lindert, P. H., & Williamson, J. G. (1985). Growth, Equality and History. *Explorations in Economic History, 22*, 341–377.

Lindert, P. H., & Williamson, J. G. (2012). *American Incomes 1774–1860*. National Bureau of Economic Research, Working Paper 18396.

Lindert, P. H., & Williamson, J. G. (2016). *Unequal Gains: American Growth and Inequality Since 1700*. Princeton: Princeton University Press.

Lindert, P. H., & Williamson, J. G. (2017). Inequality in the Very Long Run: Malthus, Kuznets and Ohlin. *Cliometrica, 11*(3), 289–295.

Lynch, J., Smith, G. D., Hillemeier, M., Shaw, M., Raghunathan, T., & Kaplan, G. (2001). Income Inequality, the Psychosocial Environment, and Health: Comparisons of Wealthy Nations. *The Lancet, 358*(9277), 194–200.

Macdonald, D. (2014, April). *Outrageous Fortune: Documenting Canada's Wealth Gap*. Canadian Centre for Policy Alternatives.

Maddison, A. (2005). Measuring and Interpreting World Economic Performance 1500–2001. *Review of Income and Wealth, 51*(1), 1–35.

Main, G. L. (1975). Probate Records as a Source for Early American History. *William and Mary Quarterly, 32*(1), 89–99. 3rd ser.

Malinowski, M., & van Zanden, J. L. (2016). Income and Its Distribution in Preindustrial Poland. *Cliometrica*. https://doi.org/10.1007/s11698-016-0154-5.

Mayer, G. (2004). *Union Membership Trends in the United States. Congressional Research Service Report for Congress.* Cornell University ILR School, DigitalCommons@ILR.

McAloon, J. (2002). *No Idle Rich: The Wealthy in Canterbury and Otago 1840–1914*. Dunedin: University of Otago Press.

McCusker, J. J., & Menard, R. R. (1985). *The Economy of British North America*. Chapel Hill: University of North Carolina Press.

Meyer, B. D., & Sullivan, J. X. (2017, August). *Consumption and Income Inequality in the U.S. Since the 1960s*. NBER Working Paper No. 23655.

Milanovic, B. (2016). *Global Inequality: A New Approach for the Age of Globalisation*. Cambridge, MA: Harvard University Press.

Milanovic, B., Lindert, P. H., & Williamson, J. G. (2010). Pre-Industrial Inequality. *The Economic Journal, 121*(March), 255–272.

Modigliani, F. (1988a). Measuring the Contribution of Intergenerational Transfers to Total Wealth: Conceptual Issues and Empirical Findings. In D. Kessler & A. Masson (Eds.), *Modelling the Accumulation and Distribution of Wealth* (pp. 21–52). Oxford: Clarendon Press.

Modigliani, F. (1988b). The Role of Intergenerational Transfers and Life Cycle Saving in the Accumulation of Wealth. *Journal of Economic Perspectives, 2*(2), 15–40. https://doi.org/10.1257/jep.2.2.15.

Morissette, R., & Zhang, X. (2006). *Revisiting Wealth Inequality*. Perspectives. Statistics Canada No. 75-001-XIE, pp. 5–16.

Morissette, R., Zhang, X., & Drolet, M. (2002, February). Wealth Inequality. *Perspectives on Labour and Income, 3*(2). http://www.statcan.gc.ca/pub/75-001-x/00202/6085-eng.html

Müller, H. G. (1984). Boundary Effects in Nonparametric Curve Estimation Models. In T. Havránek, Z. Šidák, & M. Novák (Eds.), *Compstat 1984*. Heidelberg: Physica.

Newell, W. H. (1980). The Wealth of Testators and Its Distribution: Butler County Ohio, 1803–65. In J. D. Smith (Ed.), *Modelling the Distribution and Intergenerational Transmission of Wealth, NBER Studies in Income and Wealth* (Vol. 46, pp. 95–138). Chicago: University of Chicago Press.

Newell, W. H. (1986). Inheritance on the Maturing Frontier: Butler County Ohio, 1803–1865. In S. L. Engerman & R. E. Gallman (Eds.), *Long-Term Factors in American Economic Growth, NBER Studies in Income and Wealth* (Vol. 51, pp. 261–303). Chicago: University of Chicago Press.

Nicolini, E. A., & Palencia, F. R. (2015). *Comparing Income and Wealth Inequality in Pre-Industrial Economies. Lessons from Spain in the 18th Century*. http://www.academia.edu/1752082/Comparing_Income_and_Wealth_Inequality_in_Pre-Industrial_economies._Lessons_from_Spain_in_the_18th_century

Nicolini, E. A., & Palencia, F. R. (2016). Decomposing Income Inequality in a Backward Pre-Industrial Economy: Old Castile (Spain) in the Middle of the Eighteenth Century. *The Economic History Review, 69*(3), 747–772.

North, D. C. (1961). *The Economic Growth of the United States, 1790–1860*. Englewood Cliffs: Prentice-Hall.

Ohlsson, H., Roine, J., & Waldenstrom, D. (2008). Long-Run Changes in the Concentration of Wealth: An Overview of Recent Findings. In J. B. Davies (Ed.), *Personal Wealth from a Global Perspective*. Oxford: Oxford University Press.

Oja, G. (1983). The Distribution of Wealth in Canada. *Review of Income and Wealth, 29*(2), 161–173.

Oja, G. (1987). *Changes in the Distribution of Wealth in Canada, 1970–1984*. Statistics Canada, 13-588, No. 1.

Osberg, L., & Siddiq, F. K. (1988). The Inequality of Wealth in Britain's North American Colonies: The Importance of the Relatively Poor. *Review of Income and Wealth Series, 34*(2), 143–163.

Osberg, L., & Siddiq, F. K. (1993). The Acquisition of Wealth in Nova Scotia in the Late Nineteenth Century. *Research in Economic Inequality, 4*, 181–202.

Owens, A., et al. (2006). A Measure of Worth: Probate Valuations, Personal Wealth and Indebtedness in England, 1810–40. *Historical Research, 79*(205), 383–403.

Oxfam. (2015, January). *Wealth: Having It All and Wanting More*. Oxfam Issue Briefing.

Peacock, A. T., & Wiseman, J. (1967). *The Growth of Public Expenditure in the United Kingdom* (Vol. 1). London: Allen & Unwin.

Perry, J. H. (1984). *Taxation in Canada, Fourth Edition*. Canadian Tax Paper No. 74, Canadian Tax Foundation, Toronto.

Perry, J. H. (1989). *A Fiscal History of Canada-The Postwar Years*. Canadian Tax Paper No. 85, Canadian Tax Foundation, Toronto.

Pfeffer, F. T., Danziger, S., & Schoeni, R. F. (2013). Wealth Disparities Before and After the Great Recession. *The Annals of the American Academy of Political and Social Science, 650*(1), 98–123.

Piketty, T. (1992). *Imperfect Capital Markets and Persistence of Initial Wealth Inequalities*. Discussion Paper No. TE/92/255, Suntory Centre, London School of Economics and Political Science.

Piketty, T. (2000). Theories of Persistent Inequality and Intergenerational Mobility. In A. B. Atkinson & F. Bourguignon (Eds.), *Handbook of Income Distribution* (Vol. I, pp. 429–476). Amsterdam: Elsevier Science.

Piketty, T. (2011). On the Long-Run Evolution of Inheritance: France 1820–2050. *Quarterly Journal of Economics, 126*(3), 1071–1131.

Piketty, T. (2014). *Capital in the 21st Century*. Cambridge, MA: Harvard University Press.

Piketty, T., & Saez, E. (2003). Income Inequality in the United States, 1913–1998. *The Quarterly Journal of Economics, CXVIII*(1), 1–39.

Piketty, T., & Saez, E. (2013). A Theory of Optimal Inheritance Taxation. *Econometrica, 81*(5), 1851–1886.

Piketty, T., & Zucman, G. (2013). *Capital Is Back: Wealth-Income Ratios in Rich Countries, 1700–2010*. Working Paper, Paris School of Economics.

Piketty, T., Postel-Vinay, G., & Rosenthal, J.-L. (2006). Wealth Concentration in a Developing Economy: Paris and France, 1807–1994. *American Economic Review, 96*(1), 236–256.

Pikkety, T., Postel-Vinay, G., & Rosenthal, J.-L. (2014). Inherited vs Self-Made Wealth: Theory & Evidence from a Rentier Society (Paris 1872–1927). *Explorations in Economic History, 51*, 21–40.

Pope, C. L. (1989). Households on the American Frontier: The Distribution of Income and Wealth in Utah 1850–1900. In D. W. Galenson (Ed.), *Markets in History: Economic Studies of the Past* (pp. 148–189). Cambridge: Cambridge University Press.

Potter, D. M. (1954). *People of Plenty: Economic Abundance and the American Character*. Chicago: University of Chicago Press.

Ransom, R. L., & Sutch, R. (1986). The Life-Cycle Transition: A Preliminary Report on Wealth-Holding in America, Chapter 10. In *Income and Wealth Distribution in Historical Perspective* (Vol. 1). Utrecht: Rijksuniversiteit te Utrecht, Two Volumes.

Reed, H. (2014, May 29). Piketty, Chris Giles and Wealth Inequality: It's All About the Discontinuities. *The Guardian*. https://www.theguardian.com/news/datablog/2014/may/29/piketty-chris-giles-and-wealth-inequality-its-all-about-the-discontinuities

Reeves, R. V. (2017). *Dream Hoarders. How the American Upper Middle Class Is Leaving Everyone Else in the Dust*. Washington, DC: Brooking.

Reis, J. (2016). Deviant Behaviour? Inequality in Portugal 1565–1770. *Cliometrica*. https://doi.org/10.1007/s11698-016-0152-7.

Riddell, C. (1993). Unionization in Canada and the United States: A Tale of Two Countries, Chapter 4. In D. Card & R. B. Freeman (Eds.), *Small Differences that Matter: Labor Markets and Income Maintenance in Canada and the United States* (pp. 109–148). Chicago: National Bureau of Economic Research, University of Chicago Press.

Rognlie, M. (2015). *Deciphering the Fall and Rise in the Net Capital Share: Accumulation on Scarcity?* Brookings Papers on Economic Activity, Spring, pp. 1–54.

Roine, J., & Waldenström, D. (2015). Long-Run Trends in the Distribution of Income and Wealth. In A. B. Atkinson & F. Bourguignon (Eds.), *Handbook of Income Distribution* (Vol. 2A, pp. 469–592). Amsterdam: Elsevier.

Rowlingson, K. (2012, December), *Wealth Inequality: Key Facts*. Policy Commission on the Distribution of Wealth, University of Birmingham. http://www.birmingham.ac.uk/Documents/research/SocialSciences/Key-Facts-Background-Paper-BPCIV.pdf

Royal Commission. (1979). *Royal Commission on the Distribution of Income and Wealth*. Report No. 7, Fourth Report on the Standing Reference. London: HMSO.

Rubinstein, W. D. (1979). The Distribution of Personal Wealth in Victoria 1860–1974. *Australian Economic History Review, 19*, 26–41.

Ryan-Collins, J., Lloyd, T., & Macfarlane, L. (2017). *Rethinking the Economics of Land and Housing*. London: Zed Books.

Ryckbosch, W. (2017). Economic Inequality and Growth Before the Industrial Revolution: The Case of the Low Countries (Fourteenth to Nineteenth Centuries). *European Review of Economic History, 20*, 1–22.

Saez, E., & Veall, M. (2005). The Evolution of High Incomes in Northern America: Lessons from Canadian Evidence. *American Economic Review, 95*, 831–849.

Saez, E., & Zucman, G. (2016). Wealth Inequality in the United States Since 1913: Evidence from Capitalized Income Tax Data. *The Quarterly Journal of Economics, 131*(2), 519–578.

Salmon, S. (1980). Ethnic Differences in Farm Family Land Transfers. *Rural Sociology, 45*, 290–308.

Savvidesa, A., & Stengos, T. (2000). Income Inequality and Economic Development: Evidence from the Threshold Regression Model. *Economics Letters, 69*, 207–212.

Scheidel, W. (2017a, February 21). The Only Thing, Historically, That's Curbed Inequality: Catastrophe. *The Atlantic*. https://www.theatlantic.com/business/archive/2017/02/scheidel-great-leveler-inequality-violence/517164/

Scheidel, W. (2017b). *The Great Leveler: Violence and the History of Inequality from the Stone Age to the Twenty-First Century*. Princeton: Princeton University Press.

Shammas, C. (1993). A New Look at Long-Term Trends in Wealth Inequality in the United States. *The American Historical Review, 98*(2), 412–431.

Shanahan, M. P. (1995). The Distribution of Personal Wealth in South Australia, 1905–1915. *Australian Economic History Review, 35*(2), 82–111.

Shanahan, M. P., & Correll, M. (1997, July 10–13). *In Search of Kuznet's Curve. A Reexamination of the Distribution of Wealth in the United States Between 1650 and 1950*. Paper Presented at the Conference 'Third World Congress of Cliometrics', Munich.

Siddiq, F. K. (1988). The Size Distribution of Probate Wealth-Holdings in Nova Scotia in the Late 19th Century. *Acadiensis, 18*(1), 136–147.

Siddiq, F. K., & Gwyn, J. (1991). The Importance of Probate Inventories in Estimating the Distribution of Wealth. *Nova Scotia Historical Review, 11*, 103–117.

Skott, P. (2011). *Increasing Inequality and Financial Instability*. Department of Economics Working Paper, University of Massachusetts, Amherst.

Smith, J. C., & Franklin, S. D. (1974). The Concentration of Personal Wealth, 1922–1969. *American Economic Review: Papers and Proceedings, 64*(2), 162–167.

Soltow, L. (1975). *Men and Wealth in the United States 1850–1870*. New Haven: Yale University Press.

Soltow, L. (1979). Inequality Amidst Abundance: Land Ownership in Early 19th Century Ohio. *Ohio History, 88*(2), 133–151.

Soltow, L. (1981). The Distribution of Property Values in England and Wales in 1798. *The Economic History Review, 34*(2), 60–70.

Soltow, L. (1989). *Distribution of Wealth and Income in the United States in 1798*. Pittsburgh: University of Pittsburgh Press.

Steckel, R. H. (1990). Poverty and Prosperity: A Longitudinal Study of Wealth Accumulation, 1850–1860. *The Review of Economics and Statistics, 72*(2), 275–285.

Steckel, R. H., & Moehling, C. M. (2001). Rising Inequality: Trends in the Distribution of Wealth in Industrializing New England. *Journal of Economic History, 61*, 160–183.

Stewart, J. I. (2006). Migration to the Agricultural Frontier and Wealth Accumulation, 1860–1870. *Explorations in Economic History, 43*(4), 547–577.
Stewart, J. I. (2009). Economic Opportunity or Hardship? The Causes of Geographic Mobility on the Agricultural Frontier. *The Journal of Economic History, 69*(1), 238–268.
Stiglitz, J. (2012). *The Price of Inequality*. New York: W.W. Norton & Company.
Subramanian, S. V., & Kawachi, I. (2004). Income Inequality and Health: What We Have Learned So Far. *Epidemiologic Reviews, 26*(1), 78–91.
Tanzi, V. (2011). *Government Versus Markets: The Changing Economic Role of the State*. Cambridge: Cambridge University Press.
Urquhart, M. C. (1993). *Gross National Product, Canada 1870 to 1926*. Montreal: McGill-Queen's University Press.
Vanek, J. (1963). *The Natural Resource Content of United States Foreign Trade, 1870–1955*. Cambridge, MA: MIT Press.
Velasco, G. F. (2016). *Natural Resources, State Formation and the Institutions of Settler Capitalism: The Case of Western Canada, 1850–1914*. PhD Thesis, London School of Economics and Political Science.
Vermuelen, P. (2016). Estimating the Top Tail of the Wealth Distribution. *American Economic Review: Papers and Proceedings, 106*(5), 646–650.
Wagner, A. (1893). *Grundlegung der politischen Oekonomie: 1. Theil, Grundlagen der Volkswirthschaft*. Leipzig: CF Winter, 2 vols.
Wagner, A. (1894). *Grundlegung der politischen Oekonomie: 2. Theil, Volkswirthschaft und Recht, besonders Vermogensrecht*. Leipzig: CF Winter, 5 vols.
Waldenström, D. (2017). Wealth-Income Ratios in a Small, Developing Economy: Sweden, 1810–2014. *Journal of Economic History, 77*(1), 285–313.
Walker, T. R. (2000). Economic Opportunity on the Urban Frontier: Wealth and Nativity in Early San Francisco. *Explorations in Economic History, 37*, 258–277.
Watkins, M. H. (1963). A Staple Theory of Economic Growth. *The Canadian Journal of Economics and Political Science, 24*, 141–158.
Willetts, D. (2007). England and Britain, Europe and the Anglosphere. *The Political Quarterly, 78*(1), 54–61.
Williamson, J. G. (1965). Regional Inequality and the Process of National Development. *Economic Development and Cultural Change, 13*, 1–84, Part 2.
Williamson, J. G. (1996a). *Globalization and Inequality Then and Now: The Late 19th and Late 20th Centuries Compared*. National Bureau of Economic Research, Working Paper 5491.
Williamson, J. G. (1996b). Globalization, Convergence and History. *The Journal of Economic History, 56*(2), 277–306.
Williamson, J. G. (1998). Growth, Distribution and Demography: Some Lessons from History. *Explorations in Economic History, 35*(3), 241–271.
Williamson, J. G., & Lindert, P. H. (1980). *American Inequality: A Macroeconomic History*. New York: Academic Press.

Wolff, E. N. (1987). Estimates of Household Wealth Inequality in the U.S. 1962–1983. *Review of Income and Wealth, 33*(3), 231–256.

Wolff, E. N. (1991). The Distribution of Household Wealth: Methodological Issues, Time Trends, and Cross-Sectional Comparisons. In L. Osberg (Ed.), *Economic Inequality and Poverty: International Perspectives* (pp. 92–133). New York: M.E. Sharpe, Inc.

Wolff, E. N. (1996). International Comparisons of Wealth Inequality. *Review of Income and Wealth, 42*(4), 433–451.

Wolff, E. N. (2010, March). *Recent Trends in household Wealth in the United States: Rising Debt and the Middle Class Squeeze-an Update to 2007*. Levy Economics Institute. Working Paper No. 589.

Wolff, E. N. (2016). Household Wealth Trends in the United States, 1962 to 2013: What Happened over the Great Recession? *Russell Sage Foundation Journal of the Social Sciences, 2*(6), 24–43.

Wolff, E. N., & Marley, M. (1989). Long-Term Trends in U.S. Wealth Inequality: Methodological Issues and Results. In R. E. Lipsey & H. S. Tice (Eds.), *The Measurement of Saving and Wealth*. Chicago: NBER.

Wolfson, M. C. (1979). Wealth and the Distribution of Income, Canada 1969–70. *The Review of Income and Wealth, 25*(2), 129–140.

Wright, G. (1990). The Origins of American Industrial Success, 1879–1940. *American Economic Review, 80*, 651–668.

Yalnizyan, A. (2010, December). *The Rise of Canada's Richest 1%*. Canadian Center for Policy Alternatives.

# Index[1]



[1] Note: Page numbers followed by 'n' refer to notes.



L. Di Matteo, *The Evolution and Determinants of Wealth Inequality in the North Atlantic Anglo-Sphere, 1668–2013*,
https://doi.org/10.1007/978-3-319-89773-8

CPSIA information can be obtained
at www.ICGtesting.com
Printed in the USA
LVHW02*2038150718
583816LV00014B/815/P

9 783319 897721